ORGANIZATIONAL COMMUNICATION
AND CULTURAL VISION

SUNY Series, Human Communication Processes
Donald P. Cushman and Ted J. Smith, III, Editors

ORGANIZATIONAL COMMUNICATION AND CULTURAL VISION

Approaches for Analysis

MARY LESLIE MOHAN

STATE UNIVERSITY OF NEW YORK PRESS

Published by
State University of New York Press, Albany

© 1993 State University of New York

Printed in the United States of America

For information, address State University of New York
Press, State University Plaza, Albany, N.Y. 12246

Production by E. Moore
Marketing by Theresa A. Swierzowski

Library of Congress Cataloging-in-Publication Data

Mohan, Mary Leslie, 1950–
    Organizational communication and cultural vision: Approaches for
analysis/Mary Leslie Mohan.
        p. cm. — (SUNY series, human communication processes)
    Includes bibliographical references and index.
    ISBN 0-7914-1537-6 (alk. paper). — ISBN 0-7914-1538-4 (pbk.:
alk. paper)
    1. Communication in organizations. 2. Corporate culture.
I. Title II. Series: SUNY series in human communication processes.
HD30.3.M64 1993
302.3'5   dc20   92-30247
                                                          CIP

10   9   8   7   6   5   4   3   2   1

CONTENTS

PART III

PREFACE

In recent years, researchers, consultants, and managers have become intrigued with the concept of culture as a viable approach to understanding organizations. The trend toward uncovering an organization's shared conceptualizations and hidden assumptions challenged investigators to reveal subtle, previously ignored facets of organizational life. Popularized literature lauded the functional benefits of cohesive corporate cultures, conceived by management and implanted across organizational ranks as powerful prescriptions for high performance. Some scholars, on the other hand, cautioned that cohesive cultures may not serve the best interests of all organizational constituencies. Although efficient, corporate cultures may stifle self-expression and diversity that enhance long-term organizational growth.

It became apparent, with the rapid expansion of organizational culture literature, that a careful analysis of dominant trends and approaches was in order. The burgeoning literature on organizational culture represents a wide variety of diverse conceptual and methodological approaches. Presently, there seems to be a growing trend among organizational culture researchers to reflect on the literature produced over the last two decades. This volume is indicative of the movement toward synthesis and represents a modest step in the understanding of interrelationships among existing approaches, in order to create more holistic models of organizational culture.

Several researchers have noted recently an increasing shift in the direction of multiframe/pluralistic approaches to understanding and managing organizations. The concept of 'reframing' our traditional ways of analyzing organizations has gained attention. For instance,

Bolman and Deal (1991) observed: "The trend toward more comprehensive, multiframe approaches is rapidly gathering steam and promises a challenging and exciting future for organizational science" (p. 319). Similarly, organizational culture "gurus," Frost et al. (1991) recently advised scholars to create their own "frames" for understanding this complex phenomenon. These researchers also advocated "framebreaking" if necessary in order to keep scholarly inquiry into organizational culture alive in the emerging century. Rather than proclaiming the "death" of organizational culture research, a fresh look at the legacy of two decades may indeed, breath new life into the exploration of collective identities within organizations.

As mentioned earlier, this volume represents an effort to synthesize much of the existing organizational culture literature emanating from a variety of paradigms, metaphors, and puzzle-solving strategies. The chapters examine a wide range of theoretical and methodological approaches to organizational culture and suggest ways in which some of the diverse approaches might be united to provide a more holistic view of the organizational culture construct. In summarizing and evaluating almost two decades of research, this volume seeks to suggest alternative theoretical frames to advance construct development.

Part 1 of the book integrates three dominant theoretical approaches to culture as evidenced in contemporary literature: cognitive, systemic, and symbolic. The initial chapters discuss the way in which researchers frequently combine theoretical frames and position organizational culture as a bridge between interpretive and functionalist paradigms. Chapter 1 discusses the vast array of historical and contemporary definitions of organizational culture, and provides a model of definitional components useful in construct assessment. Chapter 2 focuses in on the placement of the "o.c." construct within and across existing paradigms by examining the diverse metaphors framing organizational investigations. Chapter 3 reviews literature reflecting dominant methodological approaches, or the "puzzle-solving strategies" selected by researchers to assess cognitive, systemic, and symbolic perspectives of organizational culture. Chapter 4 examines the role of evolutionary processes in employee socialization, identification, and organizational lifestages. The role of management in the creation and maintenance of corporate cultures is considered in chapter 5.

In order to apply the theoretical concepts presented in the first portion of the book, part 2 details a field investigation of organizational culture in two large, urban universities. Specifically, chapter 6 describes a case study in which a triangulated methodology was used to assess the range and stability of cultural dimensions in organizations at two differing growth stages. The role of leadership in the process of culture creation is examined in relation to the articulation of collective vision and mission. In discussing results of the case study, chapter 7 presents two "portraits" of "stable" and "unstable" organizational culture contexts, while the final chapter sets forth a research agenda of pertinent issues relating to further development of the organizational culture construct.

The creation of this volume would have been impossible if it were not for the support of several very important individuals. First, I want to thank Rebecca B. Rubin, William I. Gorden, and Alan M. Rubin of Kent State University for their expert assistance in the initial conceptualization of theoretical and methodological models presented in the text. Many thanks to Debora Lee Troglauer, secretary, and Joseph A. Bulsys, chairperson of the Department of Communication, State University of New York, Geneseo, for their tireless technical assistance and moral support throughout the project. I also wish to acknowledge the efforts of Aaron Taylor, Tom Kenny, Michele Skrobis, Kathy Hartpence, and Jennifer Smith for their computer assistance and graphic design of text figures. Catherine Berg's research on effectiveness in corporate contexts was very helpful also. I am grateful to the staff of Strong Museum, Rochester, NY; in particular, G. Rollie Adams, president, and Susan Trien, public relations coordinator, for their willingness to share information on institutional strategic planning.

In addition, I want to express my appreciation to the editors and production staff of SUNY Press for their expertise and patience throughout this project.

Finally, a very special note of gratitude to my mother, Emily P. Mohan, for her continual inspiration and guidance.

Introduction

ORGANIZATIONAL CULTURE: THE EVOLUTION OF A CONSTRUCT

Despite the popularity of organizational culture, it still remains a phenomenon that is as yet, neither fully understood nor agreed upon.
—C. C. Lundberg

Treated sometimes with distaste and sometimes with enthusiasm, organizational culture is still with us, growing into a jungle of subtrends, approaches, and directions.
—B. Czarniawska-Joerges

Over the past decade, organizational communication researchers have embarked on a diligent quest to explore a somewhat elusive entity. In examining contemporary organizational culture literature, we find at least "two paths diverging" in an academic "wood". Explorers, armed with functionalist gear, created a stir as "corporate culture" hit the popular press in full force. A diverse group journeyed on the corporate culture path, as researchers linked arms with CEOs and consultants to investigate claims that strong ideological systems correlate highly with desirable performance outcomes including efficiency, effectiveness, excellence, and high quality (Adizes 1988; Deal & Kennedy 1982; Denison 1990; Peters & Waterman 1982). With *corporate* culture emerging as a "buzzword" of the 1980s, researchers fueled the flames with evidence that cohesive cultures exhibiting clarity regarding mission and goals served to empower organizations by facilitating employee commitment and enhancing social system stability. Media coverage showcased "excellent" companies that gained a bottom-line advantage by articulating an "inspiring" vision, and then fusing the identity of their employees with corporate mission. Bestsellers sang the praises of strong cultures that exhibit consistent patterns of shared values "from boardroom to factory floor." Value-congruent work cultures were credited with providing "a clarity of purpose and a motivating energy that makes such companies major competitive forces in any industry" (Wilkins 1983b, p. 38). Companies seeking "excellence" were advised to develop homogeneity on the essential dimensions of their corporate cultures.

Not all of the hardy explorers, however, agreed with taking the path called "corporate culture." Traveling on the "road less taken," some explorers of a critical bent began checking their compasses to assess exactly where the journey toward shared ideologies was headed. Interpretive researchers were convinced that some of the functionalist explorers had taken a wrong turn in focusing only on profit-motivated outcomes and creating generalizations regarding the efficacy of cohesive cultures. Rather than being captured as variable prey, the critical explorers suspected that culture may well be a species that bears observation as it gradually emerges in safe territory. Armed with their subjective gear, the interpretive path explorers noted that the corporate aspect of a culture represents only a single layer of a complex organizational web of native subcultures. In addition, critical investigators proclaimed that contemporary culture research frequently lacks moral grounding in the evaluation of cultural dictates that emanate solely from managerial perspectives.

As the explorers converged in the clearing to share observations, it became evident that the "paths" pursued by contemporary culture researchers reveal both promises and problems. The rumor was afoot that much of the contemporary culture research may be merely "advocacy" rather than "science" (Hitt & Ireland 1987). For example, Smircich and Calás (1987) urged culture researchers to examine and to question their contexts instead of merely providing prescriptive solutions. The glaring flaws in some studies lauding "excellent" companies included defective research design, coupled with a lack of empirical substantiation (Bacharach 1989; Carroll 1983; Johnson, Natarajan & Rappaport 1985; Siehl & Martin 1990). Deetz and Huspek (1990) pointed out the inability of most culture studies to advance beyond "micro" descriptions of the social construction of organizational reality and their failure to provide a means of evaluating different cultures without favoring one set of corporate interests. A holistic view urges development of a "macro" theory of organizational cul-

ture that accounts for competing interests. Rather than blindly praising cohesive cultures, critical theorists urge researchers to consider
the threat that looms when "ideological hegemony" assumes the
"face of power" that serves to legitimize elite corporate structures
(Deetz & Kersten 1983). As we have learned on the journey, although
organizational culture currently occupies a powerful place in both
academic and managerial discourse, both its definition and its role
remain "hotly contested questions" (Bolman & Deal 1991) inviting
further exploration.

A QUEST FOR SYNTHESIS BEGINS

Although many theorists and researchers would agree on the
popularity of an organizational culture construct, as evidenced by the
burgeoning literature of the past two decades, a wide diversity of
opinion is evident regarding the optimum theoretical and methodological stances for studying this phenomenon. Mirvis (1985) characterized researchers in the roles of "detectives," "prophets," "story-
tellers," and "searchers of the deep" in their quest to reveal shared
organizational ideology. According to Mirvis, however, the plethora
of material generated by organizational culture researchers lacks a
common paradigm and consistent methodology, thus making interpretation of findings nearly impossible. Mirvis also warned of the
identity clash that ensues "when scientists become detectives, consultants become prophets, researchers become journalists, and landlub-
bers find themselves in the deep" (p. 205). Ethical dilemmas potentially surface as contemporary organizational culture researchers assume
dual research and consultant roles, only to discover the incompatibili-
ty of disparate traditions and standards.
    In addition to ethical concerns, a lack of consensus is prevalent
regarding a definition and an optimum method for examining organizational culture. In their assessment of the current state of cultural
chaos, Smircich and Calás (1987) found the literature to be dominated
by competing paradigms. Evan (1975) attributed deficiencies in culture research to the multidimensional nature of the phenomenon
itself. Similarly, Child (1981) noted the existence of formidable problems in the measurement of cultural attributes, as well as a lack of
clarity in conceptual and operational definitions. The challenge of
assessment is exemplified in the description of organizational culture
as "a code of many colors" (Czarniawska-Joerges 1992). There is a

need for researchers to examine the rapidly growing body of organizational culture literature more closely, and to synthesize diverse theoretical and methodological approaches where possible, in order to advance our knowledge of this construct.

In the midst of paradigm clashes and methodological controversies, several researchers have called for more thoughtful analyses of the existing culture literature, in an effort to clarify its contribution to the larger body of organizational theory. In attempting such a synthesis, Pettigrew (1990) admonished academics and practitioners to view organizational culture as "akin to a Pandora's box," making no assumptions regarding its contents (p. 430). Advocating cautious restraint, Kopelman, Brief, and Guzzo (1990) suggested that the starting point of the much-needed development of an organizational culture construct should be both in providing evidence regarding its utility and in the generation of theory-based, construct-valid measures.

Some theorists position the organizational culture construct at a midpoint in an evolutionary cycle. According to Reichers and Schneider (1990), constructs progress through three distinct stages of development: (1) introduction and elaboration; (2) evaluation and augmentation; and 3) consolidation and accomodation. For the construct of organizational culture, the introduction and elaboration stage, initiated in the late 1970s, was characterized by a rapidly growing body of literature justifying and defining the construct. Presently, the construct is undergoing a second developmental stage, termed evaluation and augmentation, involving indepth critical analysis and limited generalization of existing empirical findings across contexts. The growth of literature in this second stage of construct evolution is essential, in order to synthesize and to unify seemingly diverse theoretical and methodological perspectives. Without a careful synthesis of the vast organizational culture literature, an advancement toward the final evolutionary stage of consolidation and accomodation will not occur. In advanced stages of evolution, construct definitions, research methods, and certain empirical findings become generally accepted.

This volume is positioned at a step in the second phase of construct development, Evolution and Augmentation, as represented in an effort to isolate key trends in existing literature on organizational culture, and as it illustrates the application of theoretical conceptualization in the context of a field investigation. As organizational culture "explorers" search for a common path of greater consensus regarding construct definition and appropriate methodologies, the chances for convergence will increase. Part 1 of this volume surveys the key perspectives that frame conceptualizations of organizational culture. Diverse theoretical perspectives naturally give rise to a multitude of methodologies used by researchers to assess facets of culture in organizational contexts. The first chapter provides an overview of working definitions currently in use by contemporary researchers, and it delineates the core components necessary for a thorough assessment of cultural contexts.

PART I

Chapter 1

DEFINITIONS AND DIMENSIONS OF A DEVELOPING CONSTRUCT

Organizational culture researchers do not agree about what culture is or why it should be studied. They do not study the same phenomenon.
—P. J. Frost

Even a cursory overview of organizational culture literature highlights the fact that defining this elusive phenomenon still remains one of the most time consuming, if not one of the most frustrating, problems facing researchers in this area today. Although the task of construct conceptualization may prove tedious, the process of sifting through numerous definitions that emanate from diverse paradigms may lead ultimately to more holistic analyses of organizational culture. The discovery of paradoxical frames may foster richer analyses of organizations, because researchers are forced to delve more deeply into complex and seemingly contradictory circumstances, to discover meaning in organizational contexts (Quinn & Cameron 1988). Likewise, a careful analysis of competing definitions of organizational culture may yield a more mature understanding of the developing construct. The complexity of the organizational culture construct dictates the need for definitional precision. As Schein (1990) warned, researchers should not "rush to measure things," until they understand exactly what it is that they are measuring.

Many definitions that appear in contemporary literature reveal a dual-perspective focus. For example, Denison's (1990) definition of organizational culture as "a code, a logic, and a system of structured behaviors and meaning, that have stood the test of time and serve as a collective guide to future adaptation and survival" (p. 195) contains both cause and effect elements. Schein (1990) notes that evidence for the varied conceptualizations of the organizational culture construct may be found in the examination of the equally diverse operationalizations of the construct. For example, survey research methods often elicit dimensions of culture that can be generalized across contexts, while analytical descriptive methods may examine fragments of a culture, such as stories or rituals. Other frequently used methodologies include ethnographic descriptions that provide in-depth understanding of a single context, or historical methods that permit the longitudinal analysis of a culture and its patterns over time. Finally, Schein suggests that organizational researchers, in conjunction with managers, may utilize clinical descriptive methods that allow for joint client/consultant diagnosis and prescription. The use of combined qualitative/quantitative methodologies is quite common in organizational culture research, illustrating a tendency on the part of researchers to embrace definitions spanning multiple paradigmatic views.

In approaching the challenge of defining the complex phenomenon of organizational culture, this chapter will first examine a variety of definitions, in an effort to delineate essential components of the construct. Secondly, the discussion will focus on key definitional components necessary for optimum assessment of organizational culture. Appropriate assessment procedures need to account for multiple layers within organizational contexts, ranging from abstract dimensions to tangible artifacts. Since patterns of cohesion and diversity are also important elements in understanding cultural contexts, the last portion of the chapter highlights the assessment of psychological, sociological, and historical cultural range.

A POTPOURRI OF "O. C." DEFINITIONS

Definitions of culture range from abstract *webs of significance* (Geertz 1973) to pragmatic *frames of reference*. The anthropological domain has provided a host of classic definitions that view culture as "a construct describing the total body of belief, behavior, knowledge, sanctions, values, and goals that make up the way of life of a people" (Herskowitz 1948, p. 625). The crux of cultural studies lies in analyzing the way in which a group confronts problems and challenges at a given point in its history.

Although anthropologists frequently studied "societies" in the context of national boundaries or ethnic affiliations, researchers in varied social scientific disciplines suggested the efficacy of examining the concept of 'culture' in other contexts. The point of view that a group's culture was a shared frame of reference opened the way for investigations into nontraditional groups such as "street corner societies" (Whyte 1955). When culture is defined as "transmitted and created content and patterns of values, ideas and other symbolic meaningful systems" that shape behavior and artifacts (Kroeber & Parsons 1958, p. 582), it becomes a concept that may shed light on organizational interaction. Definitions such as those advanced by Kroeber and Parsons build a bridge between macroscopic anthropological research and more microscopic sociological inquiries. From the factories of the rust belt to the computer labs of Silicon Valley, each "community" tends to develop an "identifiable character," that emerges through its unique value system (Francis & Woodcock 1990).

The study of organizational culture in an anthropological mode is based on the premise that organizations are miniature societies in which individuals are nurtured and grow. However, some researchers suggest that the "miniature society" metaphor may be inappropriate when applied to large, internally differentiated organizations that require only part-time commitment from members (Gregory 1983). For example, Wilkins and Ouchi (1983) point out that organizations rarely approach the depth and richness of anthropological cultures. Because the learning of an organizational culture occurs in adulthood and members possess alternative societal affiliations, the enacted understandings in organizations are neither as deep nor as immutable as an anthropological metaphor would envision.

Many researchers argue, however, that since members of an organization engage regularly in the process of symbolic interaction, it is probable that corporate "natives" may, indeed, create distinctly shared group identities. Louis' (1980) discussion of organizations as "culture-bearing milieux" is based on the premise that organizational contexts provide opportunities for member affiliation, resulting in the creation of "sets of shared understandings" that are salient within a distinct group. Similarly, Schein (1985) claims that organizational group "paradigms" are revealed, when researchers identify the pattern of underlying assumptions governing shared perceptions about contextual situations and relationships.

Many conceptualizations of organizational culture describe a type of centralized belief structure controlling collective meanings. Cognitive "patterning" is often a key component within contemporary definitions (Barnett 1988). For instance, Pettigrew (1979) defines culture as a "system of publicly and collectively accepted meanings operating for a given group at a given time" (p. 574). This system of terms, categories, and images aids in the interpretive process of organizational stimuli. Spradley (1972) describes culture as an information system of shared cognitions, consisting of categories used to classify experiences and interpret symbols. Wilkins (1983a) concurs that the search for an organization's culture must entail a discovery of the fundamental shared assumptions within that context. These taken-for-granted assumptions fashion an organization's "self-image," as well as its image of the environment (Broms & Gahmberg 1983).

In addition to the concept of 'shared cognitions', another important theme in cultural definitions is that of discovering the actual pattern or network through which shared assumptions flourish. Theorists such as Geertz (1973) propose that cultures are symbolic structures, or systems of shared meanings, created, sustained, and transmitted through social interaction. Geertz describes culture as "webs of significance," or a "multiplicity of complex conceptual structures" that are "superimposed upon or knotted into one another" (p. 10). In this view, an organizational culture rests in a commonly held fabric of meanings, or a unique symbolic common ground embodied in shared norms, stories, and rituals (Bormann et al. (1982). A description of culture as an enduring, interdependent symbolic system of values, beliefs, and assumptions (Schall 1983) exemplifies the thrust behind definitions grounded in the social construction of reality. It is important to note, however, that the symbolic system known as a "culture," created through the interaction of organization members, is imperfectly shared. Even in the most cohesive of cultures there will exist perceptual differences.

As we have seen, most definitions contain reference to cognitive, symbolic, and system-maintaining elements of culture. Inherent in these approaches is the idea that a distinctive conceptual map functions to guide meaningful behavior. Some researchers claim that an organization's culture can be discovered in "learned ways" of coping with experience that often involve sense-making functions or behavioral rules (Gregory 1983; Louis 1980). For example, Thompson and Luthans (1990) describe organizational culture as consisting of cognitive frames that dictate appropriate behavior, thus providing general operating norms for organizational conduct. In their view, the learned behavioral strategies come about through interactions that require organizational members to engage in a process of cognitive matching of antecedents, behaviors, and consequences that will reinforce accepted cultural norms. Other "rules" approaches to organizational culture define the phenomenon as "a set of solutions" devised by a group to confront common problems (Van Maanen & Barley 1985). In order to discover these "sets of solutions" that may be generalizable across several organizational contexts, Rousseau (1990) suggests focusing on task, interpersonal, and individual values and behaviors as the locus of organizational culture.

Overall, many definitions of culture in the literature link cognitive and symbolic conceptual components with the generation of contextual behavioral norms, in order to facilitate system maintenance. Considering the definitional diversity in organizational culture research, the next section will examine several essential components to consider in holistic analyses of organizational culture.

DEFINITIONAL COMPONENTS TO ASSESS "O.C."

In the process of reviewing the wide range of organizational culture definitions in use by researchers today, it is essential to summarize the shared components across definitions. Hofstede, et al. (1990) observe that although no consensus regarding a definition of organizational culture exists currently, several characteristics of the construct tend to appear consistently in most conceptualizations. These high-consensus components include the idea that organizational culture is holistic, in the sense that it explores multiple aspects (i.e., cognitive, symbolic, system maintaining) of an organizational context. In addition, many researchers also acknowledge the fact that organizational culture is a socially constructed phenomenon, subject to historical and spatial boundaries. Although these concepts are far from novel ones in organizational literature, their integration into a single construct provides researchers with a unique challenge.

Organizational culture, then, is a construct that may be positioned at a higher level of abstraction than the more familiar, climate concept. While the culture construct enables researchers to delve into the deeper causal aspects of an organization, climate is often seen as a surface manifestation of culture (Reichers & Schneider 1990; Schein 1990). In this view, climate is a single variable within the larger construct of organizational culture. Figure 1.1 illustrates the essential components drawn from contemporary literature, that form the basis for holistic analysis of culture in organizational contexts. First, researchers need to be aware that organizational culture is a multlevel construct comprised of perceptions regarding abstract assumptions, values, norms, and more tangible artifacts. Second, in order to assess organizational culture, researchers need to trace the range of shared dimensions within a context, in order to analyze patterns of unity and pluralism.

FIGURE 1.1
Definitional Components to Assess Organizational Culture

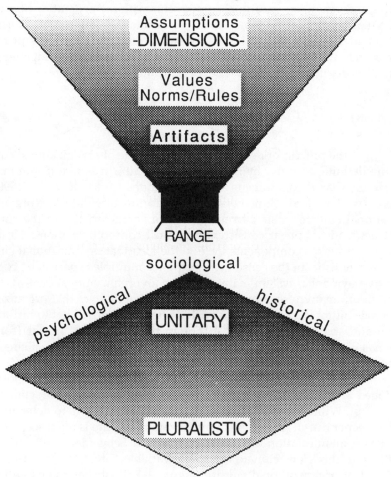

At this point, we need to distinguish between the terms *organizational* and *corporate* culture. When the term, *organizational* is associated with culture, it is understood that researchers need to examine patterns of cognitive and normative sharing across an entire context. A single organization, then, may exhibit numerous clusters of shared cultural assumptions, values/norms, and artifacts. A *corporate culture* is defined, for our purposes, as one type of culture that may be present in the larger organization. The *corporate* culture generally emanates from basic tenets of a strategic plan and is promulgated across organizational ranks by management. Although the corporate culture may touch all employees at the surface artifact level, there may be differing degrees of acceptance regarding corporate-sanctioned assumptions, values, and norms across the larger organization. The next portion of the discussion will examine in greater depth several of the components displayed in the model that are essential for holistic assessments of organizational culture.

Searching for Multiple Levels

In a summary of the state of organizational culture research, Schein (1990) delineates several consistencies in the literature. The phenomenon is recognized frequently, as a pattern of basic assumptions that are invented by a group as it learns to cope with external adaptation and internal integration problems. Schein also notes that the assumptions and the resulting strategies perceived to be valid in a particular context are taught to new members as the correct way to analyze and to confront problems. According to Rousseau (1990), "layers" of culture range on a continuum from subjectivity to accessibility. The subjective end of the continuum includes the more abstract or intangible aspects of culture, such as underlying values or fundamental assumptions. Behavioral norms occupy a middle point on the cultural continuum, while artifacts represent the layer allowing researchers the greatest accessibility.

As shown in the upper portion of figure 1.1, organizational culture is a multilevel construct consisting of assumptions, values (norms/rules), and artifacts. The lighter shading in the upper portion of the figure, denotes the most subtle, abstract level of organizational culture, *assumptions*, or the tacit beliefs that members hold about themselves, their relationships to others, and the nature of the organization. Assumptions are implicit, abstract axioms that determine the more overt organizational meaning systems (Schein 1985, 1991). For instance, Deetz and Kersten (1983) describe this "deep" layer as the unexamined beliefs and values upon which the "taken-for-granted" surface structure rests.

The next level, *values*, is distinguished by goals, ideals, and standards that represent members' preferred means of resolving everyday life's problems. The value level encompasses the socially shared rules and norms applicable to a specific context—how organizational members define and interpret situations of their workplace—as well as what "natives" perceive as constituting boundaries of acceptable behavior. The more darkly shaded tip of the organizational culture triangle represents the shared *artifacts*, or symbolic manifestations of the underlying values and assumptions. Verbal artifacts include, language, stories, and myths, while rituals and ceremonies can be classed as behavioral artifacts.

Although many investigations tend to focus on a single layer of an organization's culture, more holistic analyses provide for multilevel assessments. Contextual investigations may employ dual qualitative/quantitative methodologies to assess the entire range of layers on the cultural continuum. For example, Siehl and Martin (1988) used qualitative observation to construct a quantitative survey instrument that assesses collective agreement on espoused values, company jargon, and beliefs about practices. The multilevel assessment focuses on "values-in-use," as reflected in cultural forms and allows for systematic comparisons across individuals, employee groups, and organizations over time. Similarly, a standardized survey instrument derived from qualitative data (Hofstede et al. 1990) permits comparative analyses of values and practices across internal units and among multiple organizations.

A definition that represents a convergence of the numerous approaches summarized in this section would describe organizational culture as a *multilevel phenomenon that represents the shared, symbolically-constructed assumptions, values, and artifacts of a particular organizational context*. The collectively accepted meanings composing an organization's culture are transmitted through the process of communication and emerge as rule-governed behavior. If organizational culture is distinguished by the sharing of contextual assumptions, values, and artifacts, then an important challenge to tackle next is—devising a framework that may be used to describe and eventually assess cultural domains. One such framework consists of identifying universal cultural dimensions that cut across a variety of organizational contexts. The next section will review several generalizable dimensions, noted by previous researchers, that form the underlying structure of an organizational culture construct.

Searching for Multiple Dimensions

The practice of delineating dimensions of cultural contexts is derived from an anthropological tradition of searching for regularities both within and across cultural contexts (Kluckhohn 1951). The rationale behind searching for cultural dimensions is that, over time, distinct groups tend to exhibit preferred responses to problems posed by their internal and external environments. Thematic consistencies exhibited across artifactual, value/rule, and assumption levels of an organization form the basis of cultural dimensions. Several researchers have isolated "universal" dimensions of culture (Child 1981; Emery & Trist 1972; Evan 1975; Hofstede 1980; Kluckhohn & Stodtbeck 1961). Many of these attempts at establishing universal cultural dimensions begin at the larger societal level and are subsequently applied to the study of culture in organizations. Patterns of shared cultural dimensions may surface at differing levels of a system. Some researchers claim that cultural dimensions surfacing at the national or macro level often appear at micro levels of individual organizations or subcultures (Beck & Moore 1985; Quinn & McGrath 1985).

The claim that certain universal dimensions of both national and organizational cultures can be isolated is grounded in the idea that there are only a limited number of human problems and a limited range of solutions to those problems. The ways in which certain groups respond to life-challenges constitute collective value orientations that vary systematically across different cultures. The advantage of using a dimensional approach for organizational culture researchers is in providing the means by which to generalize across contexts. A dimensional scheme that has been applied to organizations is Kluckhohn and Stodtbeck's (1961) value orientations. This value scheme describes several orientations that surface across collectivities. Determining the range of value orientations toward human nature, the environment, time, activity, or relationships assists researchers in the search for underlying cultural assumptions both within and across organizational boundaries. Further, Schein (1990) suggests that the dimensions drawn from Kluckhohn and Stodtbeck's comparative studies provide a relevant way for organizational researchers to draw upon anthropological typologies of universal issues faced by all societies.

A *human nature* orientation (Kluckhohn & Stodtbeck 1961) refers to basic assumptions held by a society or organization about the intrinsic nature of human beings (i.e., good vs. evil). For example, in organizations, a Theory X approach to management is based on the assumption that human beings are basically lazy, while a Theory Y approach centers on the assumption that human beings are inherently motivated to work (McGregor 1960). Child (1981) notes that an organizational emphasis on subordinate autonomy and intrinsic motivation exemplifies a value orientation of the inherent goodness of human nature. Symbolic manifestations of beliefs regarding human nature might emerge in examining the language used to describe employees in the official print material of an organization, in departmental memos, or in the oral "texts" of superior-subordinate interaction.

A *person-to-nature* cultural dimension restated for organizational contexts would be an organization's relationship to its *environment* (Schein 1985). In other words, what is the basic identity or mission of the organization in relation to its internal and external constituencies? Kluckhohn and Stodtbeck (1961) suggest that the "man-nature" dimension varies from a mastery over the environment to a subjugation imposed on the organization by outside forces. Interviews with employees in corporations facing major restructuring or downsizing frequently reveal themes involving a loss of control in the face of fluctuating economic trends and massive intraorganizational change.

Organizations may be past, present, or future oriented, reflecting their unique orientation to *time*. Frequently, consultants advise that organizations work toward a moderate approach to "time," where tradition is balanced with strategic vision. For example, Peters (1988) urges corporate leaders to foster shared visions that prepare for the future, while "honoring" the past. Symbolic manifestations of time perceptions may surface in corporate slogans, mission statements, or strategic planning documents. Frequently, companies requiring perceptions of security, use images symbolizing stability, such as Prudential's "rock," in order to create the illusion of invulnerability despite social changes. Waterford Crystal's slogan, "Steadfast in a world of changing values," lauds the security provided by a strong tradition. As corporations become more attuned to social responsibility, concern for the environment has gained attention as an important time-oriented theme that is heralded in both mission statements and public relations campaigns. Often, a company's concern for the environment is framed within a future orientation—our business is not just to provide service today, but to build a cleaner, safer world for generations to come. Corporations that deal in state-of-the-art technology strive to distance themselves from "present" time orientations, claiming that their products are actually far ahead of their time, by assuming a "future is now" approach. For example, RCA teamed its nostalgic "Nipper" Trademark with an admiring young puppy protege to launch its "new generation of innovation" advertising campaign.

As organizations mobilize to greet the twenty–first century, their orientation toward *activity* is an important element to assess in the cultural mix. Values ranging from a "doing," high-action orientation to a "being," or dominantly passive, state serve to characterize organizations that either survive by "thriving on chaos" or prefer a more "laid-back" approach. Schein (1985) suggests that analyzing how rapidly problems are solved throughout various organizational levels indicates the degree of an activity orientation. In their original assessment of "excellence," Peters and Waterman (1982) stress that organizations with a bias toward action tend to be more productive. While in his later work, Peters' (1988) redefinition of excellence counsels "tomorrow's" firms to assume a proactive stance regarding change. In a "thriving on chaos" atmosphere, constant innovation, aimed at achieving higher quality, coupled with the discovery of potential "niche" markets, provide the keys for organizational survival in a "world turned upside-down."

Once researchers have pinpointed an organization's distinctive orientations to human nature, the environment, time, and activity, another essential universal dimension to consider is *relational* orientation—the patterns manifested in the relationships of persons to each other. This relational dimension ranges from "lineality," or formal hierarchical structure, to "collaterality," or team effort stressing the equality of all persons. Child (1981) suggests that on the organizational level, a minimization of hierarchy and an emphasis on delegation of authority or group decision-making characterizes a collateral orientation. A hierarchical structure in which all decisions are made by the upper echelon with little consultation constitutes an orientation toward lineality. Models of organizational structure requiring a high level of cooperation, such as Ouchi's (1981) Theory Z "clan" approach would fall on the "collateral" end of the continuum for the relational dimension. From PR slogans touting "Team Xerox," to adoption of total quality management (TQM), the focus on more consultative Japanese management styles is evidenced in the trend toward empowerment of individual employees in problem-solving processes.

Cultural analyses using Kluckhohn and Stodtbeck's (1961) dimensions include Dyer's (1985) model of culture change, in which he "mapped" the histories of several organizations across the five value orientations just presented. Evan (1975) uses the cultural dimensions scheme to develop hypotheses for three orientations (time, relational, person-nature), regarding organizational processes of recruitment, socialization, and communication. Further, Child (1981) expanded Evan's analysis to discuss all five dimensions in terms of specific organizational practices and structures.

Other researchers are also using a universal dimension approach to discover orientations that may be particularly relevant to the study of cultures within and across organizational contexts. For instance, Hofstede's (1980) extensive multinational study of IBM employees yields several independent dimensions revealing differences among national value systems. The "power distance," "uncertainty avoidance," and "masculine/feminine" dimensions of Hofstede share similar value orientations as Kluckhohn and Stodtbeck's (1961) relational, activity, and human nature concepts. Schein's (1990) "homogeneity versus diversity" dimension, which assesses how organizations perceive themselves in relation to innovation or conformity, resembles Hofstede's 'individualism versus collectivism' concept that emerged across multinational contexts.

Also, in a recent study, Hofstede et al. (1990) assesses organizational cultures across ten European organizations. These researchers describe the dimensions isolated in the dual qualitative/quantitative investigation as a checklist for variations in organizational practices. The dimensions include "process versus results," "employee versus job," and "parochial versus professional" orientations. Other factors in the study explore "open versus closed" systems, "loose versus tight" organizational control, and "normative versus pragmatic" approaches to problems. Investigations like the ones we have just discussed help refine and expand our understanding of the multidimensional value orientations that form the basis for the underlying assumptions of an organization's culture.

As the previous discussion has shown, several researchers have suggested the usefulness of identifying core evaluative dimensions in organizational culture analysis (Adler & Jelinek 1986; Child 1981; Dyer 1985; Evan 1975; Hofstede 1980). By isolating key cultural dimensions, the researcher creates a framework for analyzing the shared orientations that are consistent in the assumptions, values, and artifacts of individual contexts or that are generalizable across a number of organizations. The dimensional approach promises to be an integral part of future development of an organizational culture construct. As dimensions emerge within a wide variety of organizations, researchers can engage more readily in the process of generalization across contexts. Dimensional comparisons across organizations in the private and public sectors will yield information about value orientations that seem to be universal in all organizational cultures, and will also bring to light distinctive contextual dimensions.

So far, we have looked at the construct of organizational culture in terms of multiple levels and multiple dimensions. Once it is recognized that distinct cultural orientations give rise to varying degrees and levels of shared assumptions, values/norms, and artifacts, we need to turn our attention to the range of these salient dimensions within an organization.

Searching for Cultural Range

If we define organizational culture as a set of shared dimensions that shape the assumptions, values, and artifacts of a particular context, the next challenge lies in tracing the scope of a culture. To assess the scope of shared cultural dimensions, the researcher needs to establish boundaries of the investigation. Louis (1985b) used the metaphor of a "cultural Geiger counter" to illustrate the art and science of detecting boundaries of shared conceptualizations within an organizational context. If social scientists possessed such an instrument, they might be capable of identifying precisely the "loci" of the multiple and overlapping cultures in a single organization. Exploring the issue of "penetration" may provide a first step toward charting the range of salient dimensions within a cultural context. Penetration refers to the extent, consistency, and stability of shared meanings within a culture. Louis' (1985a) framework delineating three aspects of cultural penetration—psychological, sociological, and historical—seems to be an appropriate starting point for developing more valid measurements of an organizational culture construct.

Psychological cultural penetration assesses the consistency or homogeneity in interpretation of shared meanings in an organizational culture. Researchers charting psychological penetration focus on the extent of variation in perception of salient cultural schemata in the organization. Empirical investigations of psychological penetration might measure coorientation among employee groups regarding cultural dictates, or the degree of employee identification with the organization's mission. For instance, Cooke and Rousseau (1988) discuss "direction" and "intensity" as pertinent dimensions involved in assessing cognitive cultural domains. Direction involves the actual content or substance of cultural schemata, while intensity represents the degree of consensus on salient values and norms among organization members.

Sociological cultural penetration represents the pervasiveness of cultural assumptions in an organization. A macroscopic analysis of sociological penetration would map the range of cultural schemata beyond the individual organizational context to include the effects of more broadly based cultural systems, such as regional or national cultures. A microscopic analysis, on the other hand, might investigate how many subsystems or levels within an organization compose a distinct culture. The resulting patterns of cohesion and differentiation assist researchers in identifying unitary and pluralistic cultural pockets.

A third type of assessment, *historical cultural penetration*, charts the stability of cultural schemata over time in a particular context. Organizational researchers tracing historical penetration of an organizational culture would determine how long cultural assumptions have dominated a system. For instance, an analytic technique such as Pettigrew's (1979) sequencing of key events on timelines helps to depict graphically the patterns of cultural assumptions operative throughout organizational lifecycles. Holistic investigations need to look at all three aspects of penetration (psychological, sociological and historical) in order to provide a valid assessment of cultural range within an organizational context.

Investigators seeking to determine cultural range by assessing penetration of cultural dimensions engage in processes of "sourcing" and "bounding" in order to discover multiple cultures within organizational contexts. Louis (1985b) defined "sourcing" as locating the roots or primary sites of shared understandings, while "bounding" identifies the extent of shared perceptions. Assessing cultural range in terms of psychological, sociological, and historical penetration allows researchers to map an organization's culture across spatial and temporal dimensions, resulting in a more sophisticated level of analysis. Once the researcher has assessed the range of shared dimensions within a context, it is then possible to analyze the more general patterns of cohesion and differentiation across the organization. Identifying the boundaries of distinct subcultures will provide a graphic cultural map highlighting clusters of unity and pluralism within a context.

Searching for Cultural Patterns

Although popularized organizational culture literature with its emphasis on the benefits of fostering "strong" cohesive communities has gained prominence in business circles, many scholars question the notion that a certain type of culture may be preferable for all contexts in all circumstances. As Schein (1985) has suggested in his work on leadership, cultures cannot be deemed good or bad but depend primarily on the match between cultural assumptions and environmental realities. Individual organizational goals impact on manifestations of culture in certain contexts. A particular cultural orientation that proves successful in one organization or situation may be a liability in another case (Hofstede et al. 1990). The notion of "strong" or "weak" cultures is a concept with broad appeal, because it fills a need for consistency in organizations. However, ignoring the often contradictory nature of organizations may be disfunctional for both researchers and managers alike (Cameron & Quinn 1988). In this view, organizations are by their very nature paradoxical entities that have a simultaneous need for integration and differentiation (Lawrence & Lorsch 1967).

In searching for distinctive patterns by which to identify the scope of an organization's culture, several researchers have suggested theoretical frames conceptualizing unitary or pluralistic contextual models. For instance, the integration, differentiation, and fragmentation perspectives are especially helpful in understanding patterns of cultural unity and pluralism in organizational contexts (Meyerson 1991; Meyerson & Martin 1987). An integration approach is characterized by consistency, organization-wide consensus, and denial of ambiguity. The lower portion of figure 1.1 depicts the density of shared cultural dimensions that serve to unify or differentiate contexts. A valid conceptualization of a "strong," "unitary" culture is a high level of psychological, sociological, or historical penetration of core cultural dimensions. Conversely, an organization exhibiting some differentiation allows for the coexistence of shared assumptions with inconsistency, as represented in figure 1.1 by less density in shading at the base of the figure. In differentiated cultures, strong subcultural groups often emerge as "islands of clarity" amidst organizational pluralism. Fragmentation approaches describe organizations exhibiting a lack of clarity and consensus, coupled with an acknowledgement of ambiguity. In fragmented cultures, no clear consensus is evident.

Although many organizational culture investigations focus on a single perspective, researchers are discovering that, realistically, organizational culture needs to be assessed from dual unitary and pluralistic viewpoints. For example, in their study of the culture creation process, Martin, Sitkin, and Boehm (1985) found evidence that both integration and differentiation paradigms may be simultaneously accurate. Similarly, in her longitudinal investigation of values among three groups of professional employees, Bullis (1990) noted a transorganizational pluralistic perspective. Likewise, Martin and Siehl (1988) conclude that, paradoxically, workplace countercultures may express conflicts and address needs for differentiation while maintaining an "uneasy" symbiotic relationship with an officially sanctioned corporate culture. In their analysis of organizational accounts, Brown and McMillan (1991) stress that the potential to produce culture lies within employees at all levels of the hierarchical ladder. They argue that rather than focusing solely on "texts" produced by management levels, researchers will glean more broadly based, efficient, and realistic interpretations of an organization's culture by analyzing lower-level "sub-texts." Further, Brown and McMillan suggest that the creation of a "narrative," which represents the diverse points of view across a single context, can provide researchers with a richer analysis of an organization's cultural patterns.

When approached from a unitary perspective, cultures are conceptualized as integrative and are often evaluated in terms of organizational consistency. The use of the term *weak*, in reference to a unitary culture, presupposes that the polar opposite, a *strong* culture, can indeed exist or be created. Van Maanen and Barley (1985) note that a homogeneous culture would exist where all members of an organization face similar challenges and subscribe to a similar normative order. Likewise, in their competing values perspective, Quinn and McGrath (1985) describe a "congruent" state in an organization where the cultural forms, personal information processing styles, leadership orientations, and external demands are matched, so that contradiction and paradox appear less prevalent. According to Deal and Kennedy (1982), weak cultures exhibit a high degree of differentiation at all levels of the system, as evidenced by rituals that enact contradictory values. Highly ambiguous cultural contexts may also have "heroes" who fail to build a common consensus of what is important for business success, resulting in lower productivity. These researchers also suggest, however, that states of "incongruence" actually afford more fruitful examination of organizational systems. Creative cultural analysis often begins by identifying "weaknesses" evident within a system.

A differentiation or pluralistic view challenges unitary cultural models by stressing the idea that it is erroneous to assume that an organization has a single culture. For instance, Louis (1985b) identifies dual "loci" of culture: intraorganizational and transorganizational. Intraorganizational loci consist of alternative sites of culture within an organization, such as distinct departmental subcultures. Transorganizational loci allow "streams of culture" to flow into the organization from outside groups and influences. Intraorganizational sites function as "breeding grounds" for the "birth" of locally shared meanings. For instance, a corporate culture represents a more public type of culture developed at the top of the organizational ladder. Other intraorganizational sites at which shared meanings emerge could be dictated by structural constraints such as vertical or horizontal slices of the organization.

In a university context, strong pockets of differentiation across the campus may result from the broad range of affiliations with disciplines that vary greatly in terms of philosophical orientation. The core cultural value orientations held by a department of physical scientists may bear little resemblance to collectivities formed in the social scientific disciplines. Although cohesive pockets of differentiation emerge from the way subcultures perceive their distinct role in the traditional university mission of research, teaching, and community service, there may exist simultaneously a strong convergence on a collective vision that elicits identification across the organization.

Other challenges to the exclusive use of unitary perspectives warn that ethnocentrism increases the tendency for misunderstandings, not only in national cultures, but also in organizational contexts as well. Gregory (1983) suggests that a multicultural image of organizations enables researchers to consider both cohesive and divisive functions of culture, thus avoiding a "managementcentric" bias that often characterizes unitary cultural investigations. In Gregory's view, organizations are more accurately viewed as multiple, crosscutting, cultural contexts that change over time, rather than as stable, homogeneous, time-bound entities. As a prescription for investigations emanating from integration perspectives, Gregory advocates use of an "intracultural variation" approach in which multiple "native" views are explored. In addition, a researcher's choice of focus within cultural investigations is dependent on both theoretical and empirical grounds for the study. For example, culture might be conceptualized in one investigation as existing within the focal organization's boundaries (coterminous), while another study might consider the impact of factors that exist outside the focal organization (noncoterminous).

Holistic investigations acknowledge the paradox that unitary and pluralistic manifestations of culture coexist in every organizational context. Sackmann (1991) argues that because culture is a complex entity, it is a construct that exhibits both homogeneous and heterogeneous properties. So far, we have stressed the importance of exploring organizational culture as a complex entity consisting of multiple levels, dimensions, and layers. The next section will summarize the key considerations in defining a culture construct for organizational analysis.

DEFINITIONAL CONSIDERATIONS FOR CLARITY OF ASSESSMENT

One point of concern for organizational culture researchers centers around the idea that although many definitions currently in use reflect multiple theoretical approaches to the construct, most assessment procedures are unidimensional in nature, thereby tapping only a single level of the construct. Future assessments of organizational culture demand a more sophisticated multilevel focus that considers the scope of deeper assumptions in addition to the significance of the more accessible surface manifestations of culture. A fruitful avenue for researchers is to delineate generalizable dimensions that emerge within cultures or across cultural contexts. For instance, value orientations pertaining to human nature, the environment, activity, time, and structure of relationships may reveal distinguishing characteristics of organizational contexts or illuminate subcultural differences.

The selection of a unitary or a pluralistic perspective for contextual analysis is another important consideration for organizational culture researchers. Literature emanating from a unitary perspective tends to focus on consistency and cohesion across organizational ranks and often describes cultures as "ideal" or "excellent." Deal and Kennedy's (1982) exhortation, "in culture there is strength," exemplifies the strong causal link that unitary researchers forge between organization-wide cohesion and superior performance. Conversely, pluralistic perspectives acknowledge the existence and impact of multiple cultures, both within an organization and beyond its boundaries.

In analyzing patterns of cultural differentiation, researchers need to become more aware of the way in which certain paradoxical elements, within a context, function in producing a dynamic interplay of competing values that can either facilitate or hinder desired organizational outcomes.

In summary, it is evident that some contemporary researchers are striving for a more distinct focus in conducting organizational culture investigations. For instance, Dansereau and Alutto (1990) identify four analytic levels framing contemporary organizational culture investigations: single-level, multiple-level, multiple variable, and multiple relationship. Single-level analyses spotlight one slice of an organization's culture, perhaps the shared values and practices formed within a particular employee segment. As stated previously in the discussion on pluralistic perspectives, multiple-level analysis attempts to identify various loci of culture and to diagnose the strength, consistency, and pervasiveness within pockets of shared conceptualizations. Analytic complexity increases with multiple-variable investigations that explore correlations among factors such as commitment, satisfaction, structure, or performance and organizational culture. Finally, holistic multiple relationship analyses trace interactions among several key variables across multiple cultural levels. Presently, many organizational culture researchers conduct single-level analyses, however, future studies need to increase the precision by which culture is assessed and also strive to integrate more holistic conceptualizations of culture as a multidimensional phenomenon.

The use of a hologram metaphor is a particularly apt way of grasping cultural complexity in organizations. Czarniawska-Joerges (1992) suggests that contemporary investigations of complex organizations are similar to holograms by the way in which they capture only a small portion of a larger picture and also because they are simply representations of reality. Looking at a hologram, the point of view changes dependent upon the angle of view. Likewise, most organizational culture investigations are able to capture only a limited picture of an organizational gestalt. And, like holograms, organizational culture investigations are depictions or interpretations of reality, occasionally labeled as mere fiction. The researcher's choice of analytic angle, whether it involves focusing on a particular cultural level or structural layer, will alter the resulting "picture" of an organization's culture.

As we have seen in this chapter's discussion of key definitions evident in contemporary research, organizational culture is a construct with roots embedded in multiple paradigms. Chapter 2 will discuss in greater depth the positioning of an organizational culture construct within interpretive and functionalist paradigmatic approaches.

Chapter 2

ORGANIZATIONAL CULTURE AS A MULTIPARADIGM CONSTRUCT

*To see the same organization simultaneously as machine,
family, jungle, and theatre requires the capacity to think in
different ways at the same time, about the same thing*
—*L. Bolman and T. Deal*

An essential step in advancing our current understanding of an organizational culture construct is to ascertain its position within existing organizational paradigms. A paradigm represents an implicit or explicit view of reality based upon a set of core assumptions about alternative world views (Kuhn 1970; Lincoln 1985). Paradigms represent general perspectives, or ways of thinking that reflect fundamental assumptions about the nature of organizations (Putnam 1982). Each worldview encompasses beliefs and values that serve to guide researchers in selecting basic premises and appropriate methodologies. According to Morgan (1980, 1983), the links between paradigms, metaphors, and puzzle-solving strategies aptly describe the research cycle. Paradigms are constitutive assumptions regarding ontology and human nature that define a researcher's view of the social world, while metaphors provide the graphic images needed to grasp the workings of social phenomena. Taken together, paradigms and metaphors give rise to puzzle-solving strategies, or favored research methodologies that operationalize theoretical conceptualizations.

Distinct views of organizational reality are represented by four classic paradigms: interpretive, functionalist, radical humanist, and radical structuralist (Burrell & Morgan 1979). The paradigms reveal variations in contextual approaches and research orientations. In the view of the interpretive paradigm, organization members construct and sustain their unique social worlds through symbolic interaction. Barley (1983) links the subjective interpretive approach with an "emic" perspective, or one in which meaning emerges from members of the group under investigation. Conversely, a functionalist perspective presupposes the existence of organizational regularities that may be assessed objectively and generalized across contexts. An objectified, regulatory approach to organizations, then, dictates an "etic" research orientation that imposes meaning on a set of data. Evered and Louis (1981) contrast the interpretive wordview's "inquiry from the inside" research perspective, with the functionalist worldview's "inquiry from the outside" stance.

The radical humanist paradigm portrays an organization's members as inhabitants of symbolically constructed psychic prisons, and proponents of this view seek to alleviate perceptions of personal alienation. Radical structuralists call attention to inhibiting forces operating in organizations, in order to foster change and eventual transformation of power structures. As Putnam (1983) suggests, the radical humanist and radical structuralist paradigms might be reconfigured more accurately as distinct schools within an interpretive approach. The general thrust of the radical paradigms leans toward interpretation, as naturalistic and critical theorists seek to understand the cognitive and symbolic power structures that lead to alienation of certain organizational constituencies. Putnam characterizes this all-inclusive interpretive approach by its placement of the centrality of meaning in social action. Interpretive theorists, as a group, aim to explicate or to critique the subjective and consensual meanings that constitute social reality.

ORGANIZATIONAL CULTURE AS A BRIDGE ACROSS PARADIGMS

As we have seen from examining the numerous definitions of organizational culture used in contemporary literature, researchers have examined the construct from a kaleidoscopic array of theoretical and methodological perspectives. The functionalist and interpretive paradigms have generated two dominant strands of organizational culture research: variable analytic and root metaphoric. Within a functionalist perspective, organizations are viewed as adaptive systems created and maintained through exchange with the environment. Functioning as an adapative regulatory mechanism, corporate culture is defined as an internal variable, "something an organization has" (Smircich 1983a). Cultural studies embodying a functionalist orientation often attempt to establish an empirical link between tangible cultural artifacts or events and measurable organizational outcomes such as productivity, physical structure, or turnover (Sypher, Applegate & Sypher 1985). Studies that portray organizational culture as a key component in facilitating organizational performance (Deal & Kennedy 1982; Peters & Waterman 1982), as a factor in generating stability (Louis 1980), or as a link in engendering commitment (Wilkins 1983b) are all framed within a functionalist perspective.

In focusing attention on the collective creation of meaning, interpretive approaches describe organizational culture as a "root metaphor" or "something an organization is." Smircich (1983a) groups literature exploring the organization's cognitive, symbolic, and unconscious processes as falling within an interpretive framework. Kilmann (1985) asserts that an understanding of "the essence or soul of the organization" presupposes that interpretive researchers "travel below the charts, rulebooks, machines, and buildings into the underground world of corporate cultures" (p. 351). This archetypal journey requires a critical analysis of symbolic content in order to discover the "deep power structure" of an organization (Deetz & Kersten 1983). An interpretive approach emanating from the critical school may illuminate how an organization's symbols serve to legitimate political interests (Riley 1983). Also, cultural studies that investigate shared rituals (Pacanowsky & O'Donnell-Trujillo 1983) or enacted group fantasies (Bormann 1983) are based on an analysis of the centrality of meaning in social action.

Within a discussion of paradigmatic approaches to organizational culture, the question emerges as to the optimum theoretical worldview and methodological strategy needed for further investigation of this developing construct. Are functionalist and interpretive approaches so disparate in their theoretical presuppositions and methodological practices that a blending would prove both unwise and undesirable? Smircich and Calás (1987), for instance, view the role of root metaphoric, interpretive culture research as providing much needed opposition to the dominant positivist/functionalist paradigmatic approaches to organizational analysis. Other researchers, however, suggest that the efficacy of a cultural approach in organizational analysis is in its ability to provide an interface between functional and interpretive paradigmatic approaches. Van Maanen and Barley (1985) describe culture as a mediating factor between the structural-functionalist and interactional realms. Likewise, Louis (1983) argues for an integrative approach to organizations and suggests that a cultural perspective facilitates a more diverse and holistic approach to organizational inquiry.

Rather than viewing organizational culture as driving a sharp wedge between the functionalist and interpretive paradigms, the construct may serve a variety of philosophical orientations (Sypher, Applegate & Sypher 1985). The use of any single research paradigm may produce too narrow a view to reflect the multifaceted nature of organizational reality (Gioia and Pitre 1990). The use of combined theory-building approaches fosters more comprehensive portraits of complex phenomena, such as organizational culture. For instance, Schein (1990) advocates the use of an integrative paradigm derived from both the social psychological and anthropological traditions. Furthermore, in their analysis of paradox, Quinn and Cameron (1988) suggest that because organizations are dynamic entities, the recognition of "multiple frameworks" within contexts may be the single most powerful attribute of renewal and change.

The convergence of rational and human intuitive theoretical perspectives (Kreps 1986) also necessitates the use of both quantitative and qualitative research methodologies. Sypher, Applegate, and Sypher (1985) warn that it may be unwise to identify a cultural approach with any single methodological bent; a combination of methods may produce a broader understanding of both the human values and the strategic logics operating in organizations. Likewise, Reichers and Schneider (1990) affirm that for both theory testing and practicality, the method of choice for organizational culture researchers should be a dual emic/etic strategy. Similarly, Schein (1990) agrees that the combination of "insider knowledge" with "outsider questions" often brings cultural assumptions to the surface. Interpretive approaches are needed to discover the core dimensions of a culture from a native's perspective. Then, once the salient shared values, norms, and artifacts emerge, functionalist, variable analytic approaches can be used to assess the effects of contextual orientations. As Wilkins and Ouchi (1983) have suggested, the conflict and confrontation that may surface in the "struggle" of scientific versus naturalistic views is essential for good research.

FROM PARADIGMS TO METAPHORS

Contemporary analyses of organizational culture emanate frequently from dual functionalist and interpretive worldviews. As previously stated, the efficacy of a cultural approach in organizational analysis may be in its ability to interface paradigms. Assumptions inherent in a particular paradigm are more easily understood through metaphoric comparisons that serve to illustrate the researcher's conceptualization of an organization. Searching for organizational metaphors evident in contemporary culture investigations illustrates how researchers work from diverse sets of paradigmatic assumptions. Through an interpretive lens, for instance, organizations are often seen as texts, theaters, psychic prisons, or even instruments of domination, while through a functionalist lens, organizations might be viewed as machine-like, cybernetic, and organismic. Morgan (1986) posited that, due to their complexity, human organizations can be conceived of in terms of metaphors drawn from seemingly incompatible perspectives.

Metaphoric approaches illustrate how diverse sets of paradigmatic assumptions are often present within a single organizational context. So too, contemporary organizational culture researchers frequently explore complex contexts that reveal paradoxical metaphors. For example, Steinhoff and Owens (1989) detail several metaphoric accounts of public school culture, based on employee perceptions of their work environments. Distinctive cultural metaphors emerging from the investigation included: the Family, Modern Times, the Cabaret, and the Little Shop of Horrors. The Family culture was seen by employees as a "home," "team," or "womb." Leaders in the Family culture were characterized as "nurturers," "friends," "siblings," or "coaches," and food rituals assumed importance. Conversely, the Modern Times cultural context was perceived to be a "well-oiled machine" powered by political exigencies. The leader or "the General" in the "modern" context was often a workaholic. A Cabaret culture resembled a well-choreographed "ballet," "circus," or "Broadway show," with a "master of ceremonies," or "ring master" in charge. Finally, the Little Shop of Horrors connoted a "nightmare" or a "prison," with a Jekyll-Hyde type leader. This unpredictable cultural context fostered an adaptive style of behavior among faculty that forced them to "walk-on-eggs," in order to deal with the "cold," "hostile," and "paranoid" behavior of the principal.

Just as a single cultural context might be conceptualized by natives through diverse metaphors, researchers work from a wide variety of metaphors in their efforts to explore an organization's culture. Using several metaphors suggested in Morgan's (1986) "images" of organization, we can observe the wide range of approaches to the analysis of cultural contexts in contemporary research. As depicted in figure 2.1 this overview of contemporary organizational culture literature is framed generally within three dominant theoretical perspectives: systemic, cognitive, and symbolic.

FIGURE 2.1
Paradigms, Metaphors, and Perspectives for
Analysis of Organizational Culture

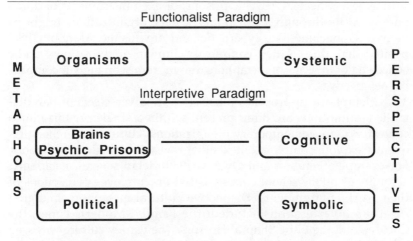

Systemic perspectives on organizational culture, emanating from a functionalist paradigm, are grounded in an "organism" metaphor and chart the way in which ideologies facilitate system maintenance across spatial and temporal boundaries. The interpretive paradigm is represented in metaphors that serve to explain cognitive and symbolic perspectives on organizational culture. First, a "brain" metaphor is indicative of cognitive cultural approaches that explore collective schemata governing "sense-making," within a distinct context. Second, a "psychic prison" metaphor is representative of cultural critiques that bring to light, the constraining or destructive beliefs, norms, and values inherent in a culture's underlying assumptions. Finally, since symbolic perspectives attribute cultural meanings to shared stories or enacted rituals, a "political" metaphor guides the thrust of studies exploring the symbolic artifacts that shape power relationships in organizational life. The following sections will highlight a sampling of organizational culture investigations that are conceptualized within the metaphoric stances of organism, brain, and politics.

Culture as Organism

The metaphor of "organism" illustrates the role of culture as a key variable in shaping the structural and functional aspects of an organizational context. An organization depicted as an organism is regarded as a system composed of subsystems engaging in an interchange with the external environment. Within this frame, an organization's culture serves a homeostatic function (Louis 1983) in growth and evolutionary processes. Also, in a systems view, an organization's culture may enhance internal socialization and task functions by reduction of uncertainty.

An organism metaphor aptly describes the functionalist-based body of organizational culture research that tends to classify cultures in terms of adjectives such as, *ideal*, *adaptive*, and *excellent*. These researchers regard organizational culture as a dynamic organism that is created and maintained by fostering a "winning" combination of variables. For example, Cooke and Rousseau (1988) used a quantitative measuring instrument to isolate generalizable attributes comprising an "ideal" culture. The "winning" combination of variables in "ideal" organizational cultures describe the contexts as achievement oriented, affiliative, humanistic, and possessing self-actualizing thinking and behavioral styles. The three empirical factors underlying Cooke and Rousseau's instrument represent three distinct types of cultures: people/security, satisfaction, and task/security. A bureaucratic, people/security cultural context is grounded in conflict avoidance and conformity, with little risk-taking. The expressive, satisfaction organizational culture values individual goals, creativity, participative management, and constructive workplace relationships. Conversely, a win-lose task/security culture rewards confrontation, competition, perfectionism, and persistence. An "ideal" culture bears a close resemblance to the satisfaction-oriented context. Kilmann (1985) described an "ideal" culture as "adaptive," or a context characterized by risk-taking, trust, and a proactive approach to organizational life. Within an adaptive culture there is a shared feeling of confidence, widespread enthusiasm, and a receptivity to change.

In contemporary organizations, the term *excellence* is often synonomous with an "ideal" type of culture. In their study of U.S. companies, Peters and Waterman (1982) identify eight practices that are characteristic of "successfully managed" unitary corporate cultures. Excellent companies possess a "bias towards action" exhibited in a willingness to shift resources to where they are needed most in order to encourage "fluidity." In addition, excellent companies are "close to the customer" in their commitment to service and in their ability to customize products and services to client needs. The "autonomy and entrepreneurship" principle describes high activity environments that foster innovation and delegation of authority. Also, excellent organizations maintain a people-oriented focus by regarding employees as their prime resource, thereby achieving "productivity through people." A clear knowledge of the company's special niche allows excellent firms to prosper by "sticking to the knitting." A "simple form/lean staff" minimizes bureaucracy, while "simultaneous loose/tight coupling" balances control with the commitment to innovation. Leaders in excellent organizations guide by cohesive values that support a clear mission and identity rather than by bureaucratic control.

In redefining the concept of excellence for the next decade, Peters (1988) stresses the need for organizational systems to adapt quickly to their rapidly changing external environment. Whereas static bureaucratic organizations in the past may have been reluctant to cut through red tape and alter formal structures, the organization that will survive in the future needs to become a flexible, porous, and *adaptive* organism. Further, Peters emphasizes the need for breaking through constraining organizational boundaries in order to engage in swift action that is designed to "constantly improve everything." Similarly, in his discussion of a Total Quality Management (TQM) approach, Atkinson (1990) reiterates the importance of matching the culture with both external demands and internal constraints. In other words, different operating units may require diverse cultures, depending on their unique characteristics and function. According to this view, excellent firms appear to be those organizations that are engaged in continual innovation as they evolve to meet the demands of fluctuating internal and external environments.

Other cultural typologies drawn from an organism metaphor are often based on processes involving market demands, human resource orientation, or styles of information processing. For instance, Deal and Kennedy (1982) constructed four generic cultures based on the degree of risk associated with a company's activities and the speed at which it obtained feedback regarding the success of decisions or strategies For example, the "tough-guy macho" culture appears in a high-risk, quick-feedback environment. By contrast, "process" cultures with their heavy concentration on bureaucratic procedures, tend to grow in low-risk environments that foster little feedback. In Deal and Kennedy's estimation, the consistency of shared values as embodied in symbolic cultural elements, such as heroes or rituals, may ensure the success of any culture regardless of style.

Other researchers have classified cultures by human resource orientation. For instance, Kerr and Slocum (1987) suggest that reward systems may forge manifestations of clan and market cultures. A clan culture, with its emphasis on fraternal relationships and strong identification with the organization, is fostered by an intense socialization process designed to inculcate a "rich" normative structure. Independence and individual initiative characterize market cultures, where a "lean" normative structure requires little formal socialization. Reward systems within clan and market environments reinforce the necessary behaviors and values related to conformity or competitiveness. Quinn and McGrath (1985) note that market and clan cultures exhibit "competing" values in terms of information processing and desirable end states. Market-oriented environments generate "rational" cultures that value logical judgement, direction setting, and goal clarification within an individual information processing framework. On the other hand, clan environments promote "consensual" cultures that value cohesion and collective information processing. Competing values are also evident in the control orientation of "hierarchical" cultures that generate formal information processing and in the intuitive methods of an innovative "ideological/developmental" culture, so concerned with revitalization and growth.

The compatibility of an organizational reward system with a type of culture is another area of interest to researchers operating from an organism metaphor. In their cultural typology, Sethia and Von Glinow (1985) isolate four cultural classifications that are characterized by varying levels of concern for people and performance. In a culture classified as "apathetic," for instance, there is a lack of concern for people, coupled with an indifference to performance. Exact opposite orientations exist in an "integrative" culture that pairs high "people-concern," with strong performance expectations. A "caring" culture is more solicitous about employee welfare than high performance, while the success-oriented "exacting" culture is dominated by a concern for productivity. As Kerr and Slocum (1987) stress, when considering the optimum "classification" for an organization's culture, the decision rests in determining which value system and subsequent style will prove effective or ineffective in terms of its support for internal and external system demands.

As we have seen in this section, researchers who adopt the metaphor of organism as a framework for their investigations generally portray culture as a key variable in the organizational mix. The organization's culture is depicted as a fluid entity that is capable of growth and development. This all-important organism has a direct impact on the function of the organizational system overall. Outcomes of a culture assume importance in this view, as managers attempt to create an optimum balance between people versus task orientation.

The benefit of an organism approach to culture is that it emphasizes the idea that culture is not a static entity but rather a dynamic force that has the potential to shape both the organization's immediate outcomes and its long-term destiny. However, a drawback of this approach is evident in the "researcher imposed" categories that are placed on cultures in order to measure outcomes and effects. Also, functional categories of contextual "types," such as excellent, ideal, or adaptive, tend to oversimplify the complex nature of the construct. Researchers typecasting organizational contexts need to recognize that they are analyzing culture solely from a unitary perspective. Future investigations can be enriched by recognizing that an organization's culture is a complex web that extends far beyond corporate levels to encompass a wide range of native subcultural structures having unique functional outcomes and growth patterns.

Just as a single metaphor is incapable of capturing organizational reality, so, too, our discussion of cultural approaches needs to examine other essential metaphors that further our understanding of the research. The next essential metaphor to consider is one that helps to explain the origin and structure of the actual assumptions defining an organization's culture. A system cannot function properly without a brain that allows for the processing of pertinent information and that generates the salient values and norms operative within a particular context.

Culture as Brain

To view culture as the "brain" of an organization, we must accept the premise that the behavior of individuals in organizational contexts is best understood in terms of their mental "sets" or conceptual frameworks. In this view, organizations are seen as "cognitive enterprises"

(Argyris & Schon 1978). For instance, Geertz (1973) described cultural patterns as "programs" that provide a "template" or blueprint for social interaction in organizations. Researchers who view culture as a cognitive phenomenon examine modes of interpretation through which patterns of meaningful action are collectively enacted (Smircich 1983d).

Underlying a cognitive approach is the belief that an organization is essentially a "body of thought, thought by thinking thinkers" (Weick 1979, p. 42). According to this definition, an examination of the organization's brain or cognitive processes would entail a close look at bodies of thought, thinking practices, and the actual "thinkers" themselves. Bodies of thought consist of recurrent schemata, the collective cognitive maps based on inferences derived from organizational experience. Schemata provide frames of reference for perception and action. For example, Neisser (1976) described three types of schemata: social system, self, and event. The "social system schemata" form a cognitive map of the history, attributes, and possible fate of an organization. "Self schemata" contain generalizations about the self, while "event schemata" represent scripts summarizing coherent sequences of events. Argyris and Schon (1978) speak of "scenarios," generated by organizational members, that reveal "theories-in-use" guiding interaction. Cognitive maps of potentially dysfunctional assumptions are also available to organization members. While Lord and Kernan (1987) note that cognitive scripts are often determinants of organizational behavior. In addition, stories may become cognitive "scripts" that provide explanations of standard operating procedures (Wilkins 1983b).

Just as an X-ray can provide a physician with a picture of sectors within a human brain, some contemporary researchers have attempted to provide detailed pictures of the components that make up realms of cultural knowledge. If cognitions are culture's core, then it may be helpful to generate specific categories of cognitions governing the shared assumptions, values/norms, and artifacts that distinguish a particular context (Conway 1985). For example, Sackmann (1991) outlines a cultural map of cognitions regarding dictionary, directory, recipe, and axiomatic knowledge. Cognitions that consist of basic descriptions or definitions unique to a particular context are included under "dictionary" knowledge. Using "directory" knowledge, cause/effect relationships are examined and attributions are made. Rules or prescriptions appropriate in the cultural context are stored under the "recipe" category, while "axiomatic" knowledge contains the underlying assumptions. The usefulness of such a map in contemporary research is that it aptly captures the multilevel nature of the culture construct. Sackmann suggests that developing a large data base of cultural knowledge profiles from diverse organizations would enable researchers to compile generalizable dimensions of an organizational culture construct.

In analyzing organizational culture from a brain metaphor, we must also consider the consequences of limiting or destructive cognitive maps that may create a type of "psychic prison." Morgan (1986) notes the urgency to "search for the hidden meaning and significance of our organizational cultures, in the unconscious concerns and preoccupations of those who create and sustain them" (p. 204). Interpretive researchers, then, need to scrutinize the popularized corporate culture analyses that dominated the literature in the early 1980s, to illuminate potentially inhibiting cultural mandates and patterns. Kilmann (1985) asserts that an understanding of "the essence or soul of the organization" presupposes that interpretive researchers "travel below the charts, rulebooks, machines, and buildings into the underground world of corporate cultures" (p. 351). This archetypal journey requires a critical analysis of how certain cognitive templates undergird the "deep power structure" of an organization (Deetz & Kersten 1983).

Crafting cultural investigations from a metaphoric stance of *brain* challenges researchers to decode the underlying cognitive structure in an organizational context. This area may prove to be one of the most fruitful for future culture research because cognitive processes appear to form the essential core of an organization's culture. It is the brain that creates and stores the abstract, invisible, deeper layers of culture, the core assumptions and dimensional value orientations that manifest as contextual norms and artifacts. Studies grounded in dual brain and organism metaphors allow for both the emergence of salient cultural dimensions and an assessment of the functional effects that such cognitions have on organizational structures.

Individual and structural outcomes that result from shared cultural assumptions may range from situations that foster greater empowerment of employees to the more constraining contexts that tend to suppress less powerful voices within an organization. It becomes useful in our discussion, then, to focus on a "politics" metaphor in order to consider the patterns of power distribution across an organizational context, in terms of an officially sanctioned corporate culture and in the more informal, native employee subcultures.

Culture as Politics

When analyzed from the standpoint of a "politics" metaphor, organizational culture becomes associated with the bases of power operating in a particular context. The shared symbolic meanings assigned to artifacts, ritualized activities, or stories reveal cultural assumptions and patterns that frequently serve to empower a particular organizational constituency. For example, interpretive approaches based within a critical school may illuminate how an organization's symbols legitimate political interests (Riley, 1983). According to Daft (1983), the value-laden, symbolic cues found in organizational objects, actions, events, and language often serve to supply information about contextual power relationships.

Symbolic stories, rituals, or visual images express the underlying organizational ideology and value system. At a very deep symbolic level, the universal psychological images known as archetypes, function as stakeholders within a collective organizational unconscious (Jung 1964; Mitroff 1983). Structuralist perspectives place member interpretations as fragments of a wider, more comprehensive mythic framework of the total organization (Turner 1977). Some researchers have attempted to unearth symbolic structures that legitimate or reproduce dominant organizational concerns, while restricting less powerful constituencies (Mumby 1987). For instance, Riley (1983) analyzed organizational symbols in an effort to determine master structures that form political images.

In organizational life, constituencies regularly engage in attempts to "gain control" of symbolic aspects of a culture. Boje, Fedor, and Rowland (1982) speak of "myth-making" in terms of its ability to maintain political interests in contexts exhibiting a high degree of uncertainty. Groups or individuals seeking power in the organization will attempt to alter the form and content of the organizational symbolic field. For example, the management of "sagas" or stories may serve to redefine the roots and recast the history of an organization. Corporate culture literature provides guidelines for how superiors may strengthen their bases of power through the molding an employee's perception of the organizational culture. For instance, Schein (1985) envisioned an essential function of leadership to be in the "manipulation of culture." This "cultural manager" possesses the ability to provide an external symbolic framework for the organization. Likewise, Burns (1978) claims that leaders who provide viable and consistent symbols possess the ability to unify disparate elements within an organization into a meaningful gestalt, thereby aiding the assimilation process.

This transformational leadership attempts to shape the motives, values, and goals of employees, and it functions to reconcile psychological contradictions between cognitions and experiences. Leaders attempting to influence a culture often identify salient cognitions and themes and then reinforce familiar norms or values. At times, however, organizational leaders will attempt to establish a new symbolic cultural vision, often as a reaction to an event requiring imminent resolution. Lundberg (1985) notes that this "revisioning" should be followed by planned interventions to induce, manage, and stabilize the new vision. Managerial intervention can occur at several symbolic levels of the organizational culture: artifacts, values, or norms. Examples of artifact-level intervention might be decor changes or the use of new jargon. According to Lundberg, the normative level of organizational culture can be managed through the manipulation of such elements as content of training programs, criteria for personnel selection, and changes in work design. The value-level manifests itself in slogans, logos, new leaders, or statements of corporate philosophy. Lundberg stresses however, that for managers to achieve an optimum amount of cultural change, their interventions should cross all levels (artifacts, values, norms) of cultural meaning and should be consistently and redundantly applied.

One of the most graphic examples of political use of cultural ideologies is a trend in management involving the creation of corporate cultures based on military principles. Garsombke (1988) identifies militarism as a distinct type of corporate culture in which managers adopt military principles as their own beliefs and then formulate organizational assumptions, goals, and plans around military concepts, behaviors, myths, and language. The adoption of this metaphor by an organization necessarily entails both benefits and liabilities. For instance, the benefits of an emphasis on discipline, group solidarity, and systematic planning could be outweighed by such factors as an absence of innovation, limited perspectives, and authoritarian control. The merger of the militaristic culture's more positive elements with humanistic approaches may produce a blended cultural schema that could prove beneficial in certain contexts. However, a culture based on corporate militarism would position the base of power firmly in the high ranks, providing little opportunity for subordinates to share responsibility.

The concept of management through manipulation of an organization's symbolic structure raises ethical considerations that involve the impact of workplace culture on the human character. For example, Deetz (1985) cautioned prospective "culture managers" to consider the potential effects of planned innovations on human beings within that context. In the critical view, conceptual systems need to be designed to enable full expression and representation of all organizational constituencies. Recent studies have suggested that greater employee freedom of speech may actually enhance organizational commitment and satisfaction (Gorden & Infante 1991). Likewise, Adams and Ingersoll (1985) encourage illuminating the dominant "managerial metamyth," or a pronounced bias toward rational and technical values, such as efficiency and predictability, that may function to suppress the symbolic systems of disenfranchised subcultural groups. Cultures that exhibit more even power distribution across organizational ranks, such as the "clan" model (Ouchi 1980), may point the way toward a solution to ethical dilemmas. A "politics" metaphor, then, adds a dimension to cultural analyses that is ignored frequently in contemporary studies—how an organization's core cultural dimensions facilitate ethical distribution of power. With increased interest in corporate responsibility and ethics, the politics metaphor may assume more prominence in conceptualizing culture in future research investigations.

This discussion has delineated three metaphor-based perspectives that emerge in the analysis of contemporary organizational culture literature. Metaphorically, organizations and their cultures can assume the properties of organisms, brains, or political entities. Paradoxically, a more fitting metaphor for an organization's culture may be that of a "prism" that reflects, simultaneously, elements of the systemic, cognitive, and symbolic aspects of organizational reality. Before embarking on an organizational culture investigation, researchers need to clarify their stance regarding metaphoric conceptualization of the context that they are exploring. Most current cultural investigations reflect a single metaphoric stance; however, researchers need to be open to the ways in which combined metaphoric approaches may allow for an enhanced understanding of interrelationships among organizational elements. Future investigations will reveal a heightened sensitivity regarding the use of combined perspectives and diverse metaphors in order to further our understanding of how culture manifests and operates within the organizational gestalt.

So far, we have discussed a variety of issues surrounding the definition of an organizational culture construct and its placement as a bridge across interpretive and functionalist paradigms. The metaphors that emanate from dual paradigms allow culture to be simultaneously conceptualized as organism, brain, or political entity. These three diverse metaphors give rise to a variety of puzzle-solving strategies, methodologies that allow for assessment of the systemic, cognitive, and symbolic aspects of culture in organizational contexts. Chapter 3 makes the transition from metaphor to methodology as it presents a variety of contemporary organizational culture investigations.

Chapter 3

CONCEPTUAL FRAMES FOR ASSESSMENT OF ORGANIZATIONAL CULTURE

The relative scarcity of work guided by multiple
perspectives makes organizational research an
unproductively fractionated endeavor. Singular
approaches oversimplify the complexity of human
organization.
—L. Bolman and T. Deal

The challenge of assessing organizational cultures is rooted in a researcher's ability to accept the paradoxical nature of this complex phenomenon. To explore organizational culture in simultaneous roles of root metaphor and systemic variable demands a more holistic theoretical conceptualization and methodological operationalization of the construct. If organizational culture "mediates between structural and individual interpretive realms" (Van Maanen & Barley 1985), then researchers are obliged to consider dual cause-effect approaches to assessment.

This chapter provides a sampling of several puzzle-solving strategies (Morgan 1980) found in contemporary organizational culture literature. The strategies used for assessment emerge naturally from three dominant theoretical frames: systemic, cognitive, and symbolic. As figure 3.1 illustrates, each frame outlines an optimum method for answering relevant questions about organizational culture. Functionalist-based, systemic approaches generally seek to discover the range, structure, and function of organizational culture as a key variable and then to assess its effect on the overall organism. Researchers conducting systemic investigations may use quantifiable measures, such as organizational audits, in order to explore interrelationships among key variables.

On the other hand, a cognitive framing of organizational culture permits an exploration of collective schemata that form the basis of sense-making within a distinct context. Researchers operating from cognitive frames frequently use qualitative methods to surface collective mental maps, constructs, or scripts and then apply quantitative techniques to assess congruence within an organizational context. The significance of cultural congruence within a particular context raises an interesting question for researchers using symbolic frames. A symbolic frame permits the interpretation of shared stories or enacted rituals created through organizational interaction. Critical techniques become essential in analyzing root metaphors, stories, rituals, or visual images. In addition, researchers need to consider the significance of symbolic artifacts in terms of power distribution among dominant corporate cultures and subcultures.

FIGURE 3.1
Multiframe Approach to Organizational Culture

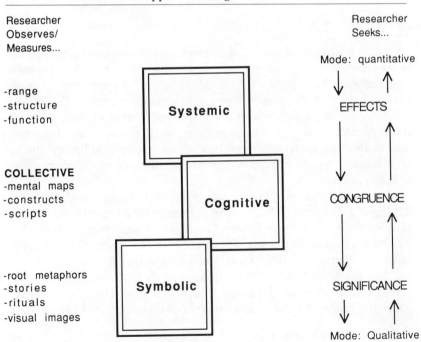

Each conceptual approach "frames" or focuses primarily on one aspect of the organizational culture construct. However, as the overlapping picture frames in figure 3.1 suggest, researchers frequently allow for intersection of conceptual frames by using a combination of approaches—the result is often a more holistic picture of organizational contexts. This chapter will review assessment strategies that emerge from the intersection of systemic, cognitive, and symbolic frames. The puzzle-solving strategies include the use of dual quantitative/qualitative methodologies in order to assess functional effects, level of congruence, and significance of organizational cultures.

SYSTEMIC FRAME—DEPICTING THE SCOPE OF A CULTURE

When a researcher imposes a systemic frame on a context under investigation, organizational culture becomes a variable that can be measured. The object of such investigations is to trace the range, structure, and function of an organizational culture variable in an effort to determine its effect. Quantitative assessments are used frequently to chart the sociological and historical range of organizational cultures. The following section reviews several contemporary research investigations emanating from a systemic frame approach.

Sociological Cultural Range—Assessing Structural Patterns

A common thread throughout structural-functional based research is the search for cultural patterns that serve homeostatic functions in the overall system. O'Toole (1979) suggests that an audit of a system's structural aspects will ultimately reveal cultural patterns. This audit generally includes a description of internal stratification, the height of an organizational hierarchy, and interaction patterns in horizontal and vertical strata. An audit frequently maps informal patterns of social relationships, the system of sanctions, and the normal career paths of individuals over time. According to O'Toole, the amassing of such data allows the researcher to grasp a holistic organizational picture while allowing cultural patterns to emerge. A similar approach is reflected in the Organizational Culture Survey (Glaser, Zamanou & Hacker 1987) that charts information flow and linkages in areas of teamwork, conflict, supervision, and decision making. A drawback of this type of organizational assessment is that often, researchers fail to distinguish between elements that compose a climate construct and elements that specifically describe a culture construct.

Conducting a systemic audit of dominant values and norms, however, enables organizational culture researchers to uncover the presence of diverse subcultures across employee ranks. Tracing patterns of shared values among distinctive subcultures can confirm whether a stable unitary culture actually exists. As Van Maanen and Barley (1985) have suggested, organizational culture is a "shadowlike entity" that can be identified as "the intersection of subcultural interpretive systems" (p. 38). If there is much overlap and tight clustering among subcultural belief systems, the researcher may have evidence for the existence of a strong unitary organizational culture. However, if the intersection among subcultural belief systems is minimal, researchers need to be cautious about claims that a unitary culture actually exists. Although organizational leaders may perceive unification throughout the ranks, the presence of cohesive subcultures may serve to either challenge or reinforce the norms and values of an "officially sanctioned" corporate culture.

The study of organizational subcultures provides a clearer understanding of the overall cultural patterning within a system. An organizational subculture is defined as a "subset of an organization's members who interact regularly with one another, identify themselves as a distinct group, share a set of problems, and routinely take action on the basis of collective understandings unique to the group" (Van Maanen & Barley 1985, p. 38). According to Reynolds (1987), each layer of the "cultural onion" is affected by a multitude of variables, such as social context and channels of communication. In tracing these differences in cultural patterns then, researchers may examine distinct types of subcultures that arise across the organization. For example, Martin and Siehl (1988) identify three patterns of subcultures: enhancing, orthogonal, and countercultural. The *enhancing* subculture exhibits a stronger adherence to core organizational values than other units. Although an *orthogonal* subculture accepts core organizational values, it also maintains distinctive group values. On the other hand, the core values of a *counterculture* pose a challenge to dominant organizational norms.

A viable way to chart diversity among subcultural groups is to identify areas where values may clash across a system. For example, Quinn and McGrath (1985) propose a "competing values" perspective that differentiates among four distinct types of cultures: rational, ideological, consensual, and hierarchical. These four cultural systems arise in response to internal and external environmental demands. A *rational* cultural system emphasizes pursuit of objectives, productivity, and efficiency, while an *ideological* culture values intuitive insights, invention, and risk-taking. The *consensual* culture promotes values of support and concern, in order to achieve high levels of relational maintenance, cohesion, and morale. In a *hierarchical* culture, the acquisition of technical knowledge, factual analysis, and execution of regulations are fostered in order to achieve stability and control. A culture audit of a complex organization may reveal competing values in the rational, ideological, consensual, and hierarchical orientations of subcultures that compose the system.

The competing values approach also assists researchers in pinpointing links between internal organizational culture and the larger societal culture. For example, Beck and Moore (1985) traced layers of "nested" systems across national and organizational cultures. By using a multiple methodology involving critical incident interviews and mail questionnaires, these researchers linked metaphoric imagery in Canadian culture with the managerial culture of a local bank. The dominant cultural themes identified at the macro-level of the national culture were replicated in modified forms at micro-levels, such as superior-subordinate dyadic systems within the organization.

Investigations that assess sociological range focus on structural patterns of culture that arise as a response to internal and external environmental demands. Audits that assess multiple layers of a complex organization assist researchers in grasping the broad picture of cultural patterns. Subcultures, identified by their distinctive value orientations, help to reveal patterns of cultural unity and diversity across organizational ranks. Systemic structural patterns, however, are not frozen in time but are, rather, in a continual state of growth and flux. Therefore, we turn to another important aspect of viewing cultural patterns in a systemic frame, the evolution of organizational structures over time.

Historical Cultural Range—Assessing System Functions over Time

Just researchers craft investigations to delineate structural boundaries of cultural systems, they may also chart the functions of culture in organizational growth. The concept that sets of beliefs and behaviors arise and are transformed in response to changing environmental conditions prompts researchers to examine cultures as historical records of a collective's response to problems posed by its environment (Harris 1981; Radcliffe-Brown 1952). One way that researchers explore historical range is by reconstructing the historical evolution of an organization. For example, Pettigrew (1979) advocates research designs that graphically depict the sequence of social dramas in an organization's history. His longitudinal-processual study of a private British boarding school focuses on key turning points throughout the life cycle of the organization. Pettigrew points out that major structural changes within an organization prompt changes within the cultural system. Overall, in the evolutionary process, culture fulfills functions of integration, control, and commitment.

In order to assess the effects of an organization's culture on system growth and maintenance, researchers may reconfigure cultural artifacts, such as stories or rituals, as variables and measure them according to their functional outcomes. For instance, Dandridge, Mitroff, and Joyce (1980) identify the functions of symbolic artifacts as descriptive, energy controlling, and system maintaining. In organizational socialization, symbolic artifacts assume an energy controlling mode as they function to attract and inspire new members while repelling "undesirable outsiders." In addition, emotionally charged organizational symbols tend to increase or decrease tension by facilitating venting of feelings. For instance, Kreps (1983) notes that a "well-developed" organizational culture exhibiting member solidarity and strong identification serves to facilitate interpretation and response. Similarly, Schein (1990) attributes a culture's "tenacity" to its "anxiety-reducing" functions, thus providing a group "defense mechanism." Specifically, organizational stories function as control mechanisms affecting organizational decisions, transmitting shared values, and increasing commitment (Wilkins 1983b). The organization's culture, as represented by symbolic artifacts, serves a number of homeostatic functions over time to facilitate system growth.

The overlay of a systemic frame for exploring cultural phenomena is helpful to researchers in charting the range, structure, and function of organizational cultures. Puzzle-solving strategies to assess sociological range are generally structural audits that reveal cultural subsystems of competing values across the organization. In addition, researchers explore historical range within organizational contexts by creating time lines that document the longevity of salient cultural assumptions and by determining how cultural artifacts affect system function and growth. In order to assess effects, researchers may measure certain aspects of an organization's culture, such as stories or rituals, as variables. As viewed through a systemic frame, an organization's culture encompasses a comprehensive scope of structural and functional patterns. While the systemic frame provides a macro-view of interrelationships, a cognitive frame is needed to focus in on a micro-view that explores the ways in which individuals create and process cultural assumptions

COGNITIVE FRAME: CAPTURING CULTURAL CONGRUENCE

A cognitive frame draws the researcher into an assessment of psychological penetration, the extent of congruence regarding core cultural dimensions. Because shared cognitive schemata form the basis of any organizational culture, Schein (1985) urges researchers to identify the "paradigm" or the group of common conceptualizations essential for membership in an organization. This paradigm consists of shared modes of perceiving situations and relationships. Further, Schein suggests that the amount of consensus regarding organizational schemata indicates whether a coherent cultural paradigm exists in a particular context. By charting the cognitive schemes used in organizations, researchers can also pinpoint conflicts between certain subcultures and even speculate on the reasons for differing perceptions within organizational milieu. The puzzle-solving strategies that appear in cognitive frame investigations frequently allow for convergence of qualitative and quantitative methods. Qualitative techniques permit core cultural constructs to emerge from native perceptions, while quantitative techniques enable an assessment of congruence on core constructs among organizational groups.

Psychological Cultural Range—Seeking Collective Maps

Cognitive-based methodologies for assessing cultural assumptions are grounded in the belief that organizations are composed of subjective constructs "housed" in the minds of members. Wacker (1981) devised a method to diagnose the "collective cognitive infrastructure" of an organization by eliciting the constructs most commonly used by employees to make sense of their environment. The basic analytic unit in assessment is the "construct," an abstract characterization used by individuals to classify environmental stimuli (Kelly 1955). Wacker's method of collective construct assessment adapted Kelly's repertory grid to the organizational context. The grid aids in the assessment of an employee's cognitive constructs regarding coworkers, jobs, specific work activities, and technical system components. Wacker synthesized twelve individual grids charted by members of a particular organization into a collective "map" displaying the shared constructs, what researchers in a cognitive frame would term "organizational culture."

Another method of unearthing shared constructs of organization members is to focus on how individuals and groups draw inferences about cause-effect relationships. In their study of the Utrecht Jazz Orchestra, Bougon, Weick, and Binkhorst (1977) created "cause maps" of both individual and collective schemata in order to display graphically the causal links among factors operating in the organizational context. Through interviews with organization members, Bougon, Weick, and Binkhorst compiled a list of factors having particular relevance to a culture or subculture. Individuals ranked the factors according to importance and also charted causal relationships existing among the variables. The researchers compared individual "cause maps" for areas of perceptual convergence or divergence across the entire group. They reduced the complexity of synthesizing numerous perceptual maps by a sequential clustering of patterns. The synthesized map is usually shown to organization members to give them a broader perspective regarding the sense-making functions at work in the macro-system. Cause maps result from overlapping systemic and cognitive frames to reveal organizational structure created by construct sharing.

Finding Individual/Organizational Congruence

The goal of cognitive cultural investigations involves not only the identification of salient constructs, but also an assessment of the degree of congruence between individual conceptualizations and core organizational schema (Enz 1988). For instance, Liedtka (1989) posits that the nature of conflict experienced by an organization member who is confronted with a difficult decision tends to vary according to the interplay of value congruence at individual and organization-wide levels. In order to gauge an accurate measurement of congruence within organizational contexts, Barnett (1988) recommends use of the Galileo System as a theoretical basis for measurement of collective consciousness. The method involves isolating a domain of critical concepts/symbols composing an organization's culture and then engaging organization members in a series of pair comparisons. Analysis of spatial coordinates provides a graphic representation of the organizational culture's meaning system. The direct magnitude estimates used in this method allow for greater flexibility than traditional free-choice scales and isolate the degree of inconsistency within an organization's cognitive cultural system.

Another important aspect of congruency research is the assessment of the "fit" between an individual's values and organizational values. Using longitudinal data from accounting firms and government agencies, O'Reilly, Chatman, and Caldwell (1991) validated the Organizational Culture Profile (OCP), a survey instrument designed to assess person-organization fit. Using current literature, the researchers compiled value statements describing orientations that may be present in a variety of organizational cultures. The value statements include such attributes as: innovation, stability, respect for people, team orientation, and aggressiveness. Through the use of Q-sort profiles, employees can identify a range of relevant values for the organization, as well as the scope of individual preferences. Person-culture fit is calculated by correlating the profile of organizational values with the profile of individual preferences. According to these researchers, employees are generally more satisfied and possess higher levels of commitment in organizational cultures perceived as having values similar to their own.

Other cognitive frame approaches to organizational culture trace congruency regarding behavioral norms. For example, Cooke and Rousseau's (1988) Organizational Culture Inventory (OCI) assesses the ways that organization members are expected to think and behave, relative to task-oriented, interpersonal, and individual values and behaviors. The OCI is a configuration of individual interpersonal and task-related styles (Cooke & Lafferty 1986; Lafferty 1973) that collectively represent cultural preferences. The dominant thinking styles reflected in individual and organization-wide profiles represent styles perceived to be necessary for success within a particular context. The OCI measures the direction and intensity of perceived organizational norms and expectations. Similarly, the Kilmann and Saxton (1983) Culture Gap Survey detects differences between desired versus actual organizational norms. Configurations of "gaps" provide a graphic cognitive map revealing patterns of perceptual diversity regarding cultural norms. Often, such analyses are used in organizational consultation as a basis for planning and change processes.

In overlaying systemic and cognitive frames, researchers work to unearth a set of shared conceptualizations and then to assess stability of the culture across organizational ranks. For instance, Harris and Cronen (1979) posit that an organization's culture can be analyzed by identifying its collectively defined "master contract," a cognitive construct enacted by organization members, and operating within two dimensions: image and rules. According to Harris and Cronen, an organizational image is composed of three analytic levels: constructs used to define the organization, beliefs about the organization, and ideal goal states for the organization. Based on this "image," organization members negotiate rules that define appropriate behavior within the context. The image component of the master contract may be viewed as cognitive schemata, and the rules generated by the contract provide for system maintenance. In their case study of an academic department, Harris and Cronen explore the nature and extent of consensus on organizational image and perceived latitudes of accepted behavior. By assessing the constructs that individuals use to define their organization, researchers may then determine if congruence regarding organizational image facilitates system coordination.

The master contract concept generated other cognitive-based investigations that assess coorientation regarding salient work group rules. In an effort to highlight cultural differences between units in large organizations, Schall (1983) analyzed two subcultures to determine operative workplace rules. The multiple method study reveals a dichotomy between formally sanctioned rules of top management and operative rules of the subcultures, however, the perceived and enacted rules of subcultural groups remain consistent with individually espoused values and norms. Using observation and interview techniques, Van Ess Coeling and Wilcox (1988) elicited operative rules in two nursing units. Categories for rule-governed behavior include situations such as working together, giving direction, following established procedures, use of time, and implementing change. Analysis of group perceptions regarding appropriate norms reveals two distinct work-unit cultures, whose differences have an impact on nursing administrative decisions.

So far, this discussion has focused on use of systemic and cognitive frames to assess the organizational culture. Working from a systemic frame, researchers trace the range of sociological penetration by charting the structure of unitary and pluralistic boundaries within the organism. In addition, the pervasiveness over time of cultural assumptions, values/norms, and artifacts represents the range of historical penetration. With the addition of a cognitive frame, the researcher is able to isolate shared cognitive constructs and then map the psychological penetration of culture by using a number of methods that assess congruence. As systemic and cognitive frames intersect, researchers are able to explore the ways in which cultural congruence facilitates system functioning. Addition of a third frame, discussed in the next section, calls attention to assessing the significance of symbolic manifestations through a critical analysis of cultural contexts.

SYMBOLIC FRAME: REVEALING SIGNIFICANCE

So far, we have discussed frames that enable researchers to assess the effects of cultural congruence on organizational function and structure. The third frame presented in this chapter adds a very important aspect to the concept of assessment—the significance of symbolic cultural components. The symbolization process is one in which "human beings vest elements of their world with a pattern of meaning and significance which extends beyond its intrinsic content" (Pondy et al. 1983, p. 5). By analyzing symbols that are significant to organizational members, interpretive researchers may delve beneath the objective surface of mundane activities into the deeper, ideological structure. The shared meanings assigned to artifacts, ritualized activities, or stories by natives reveal cultural assumptions and patterns. From a functionalist perspective, organizational symbols facilitate key organizational processes, such as an employee's interpretation and understanding of an organization as well as their identification with the collective effort. According to Daft (1983), the value-laden, symbolic cues found in organizational objects, actions, events, and language supply information about contextual power relationships, normative behavior, member commitment, and motivational levels.

An organization's symbolic field is shaped along two dimensions of reality: diachronic and synchronic. The diachronic or "syntagmatic" dimension refers to the systematic arrangement of organizational history over time by creating reference points in a "symbolic universe " (Berg 1985). This codified, "reinterpreted" perception of historical events provides organization members with useful information for interpretation of present experience. The synchronic or "paradigmatic" dimension operates at the deeper, root metaphoric level, by providing organization members with a pattern of underlying assumptions regarding organizational significance. This "dominant myth" is the fundamental generator of organizational values and resulting policies and practices. At a very deep symbolic level, the universal psychological images known as archetypes, function as stakeholders within a collective organizational unconscious (Jung

1964; Mitroff 1983). Structuralist perspectives place member interpretations as fragments of a wider more comprehensive mythic framework of the total organization (Turner 1977). Some researchers attempt to unearth symbolic structures that legitimate or reproduce dominant organizational concerns while restricting less powerful constituencies (Mumby 1987). Symbolic perspectives, then, may range from the analysis of tangible outward manifestations of a culture to an interpretation of subconscious mythic structures.

The term *organizational symbolism*, then, refers to those aspects of an organization that members use to reveal unconscious feelings images and values inherent in the context (Dandridge, Mitroff & Joyce 1980; Morgan, Frost & Pondy 1983). Symbolic stories, rituals, or visual images express the underlying organizational ideology and value system (Dandridge 1983). Within a symbolic frame, organizational culture is viewed as "something an organization is," and meanings emerge from the experience of natives, rather than being imposed by an objective researcher. However, in analyzing organizational culture research that draws on a symbolic perspective but overlays a systemic frame, "symbols" as variables are identified and then quantified in order to measure effects. In synthesizing the wide variety of symbolic investigations in contemporary literature, we need to make the distinction between studies that assess the effects of researcher-determined cultural symbols, used as key variables, and investigations that allow native-generated symbols to emerge and define the context. In the following discussion, we will look at a variety of studies with roots in dual functionalist/interpretive perspectives that illustrate how symbolic significance is interpreted and assessed by analyzing organizational actions and language.

The Role of Drama in Organizational Culture

A dramatistic perspective aids in the understanding of the symbolic activities known as organizational rites and rituals. Goffman (1956) portrays "everyday life" as a series of vignettes in which actors collectively create social dramas for audiences. Within organizations, individuals join with a collectivity to enact ceremonies that fulfill specific functions for both actors and audiences. For instance, Trice and Beyer (1984) describe these workplace performances as "rites," dramatic, scripted activities "that consolidate various forms of cultural expressions into one event" (p. 655). They added that rites are carried out through social interaction for the benefit of an audience. The typology proposed by Trice and Beyer includes rites of passage, degradation, enhancement, renewal, conflict reduction, and integration. As these categories illustrate, rites normally facilitate transitions throughout an organization's life cycle or employee's career path and commonly involve major role changes, such as hiring, firing, or promotion. In addition to formalized rites, significant "rituals" often emerge in organizational contexts as a result of repeated "everyday" behavior (e.g., a coffee break).

Using an ethnographic methodology to investigate rituals, researchers can view culture as an enacted symbolic process, rather than a collection of quantifiable variables determined by the researcher. Pacanowsky and O'Donnell-Trujillo's (1983) observation of the "ordinary" world of police officers reveals five cultural dramas: ritual, passion, sociality, politics, and enculturation. A task ritual might consist of the opening of the daily mail, and a social ritual could involve a midmorning chat at the drinking fountain. Rituals specific to a particular organizational context, such as police stations, may describe an event, like the daily roll-call of the officers. A performance of passion constitutes the glorification of ordinary routine, as in the writing a parking ticket to represent an officer's unflinching enactment of duty.

Performances of sociality include expected pleasantries or well-known "insider" jokes. In political performances, organizational members engage in interaction that clearly aligns them with certain allies in order to achieve a more influential status. Finally, the performance ritual of enculturation facilitates the socialization process. In a police context, an enculturation ritual would involve a veteran of the force driving around town to orient a rookie cop to the familiar scenes of a typical beat. By interpreting the symbolic significance of contextual rites and rituals, researchers can better understand how formal and informal behavior shapes cultural perceptions.

The Role of Language in Organizational Culture

Most of the symbolic systems used in organizations have some linguistic base. For instance, in the enactment of rites and rituals, symbolic meaning is conveyed not only through specific actions, but also in the oral "scripts" constructed by organizational actors. Evered (1983) suggests that the language used by organization members reveals their unique world view. Similarly Frake (1972) claims that researchers can discern how individuals interpret their world of experience by analyzing the way they talk about it. In addition, cognitive constructs pertaining to organizational culture are likely to be revealed in the speech of organization members. This section will review several investigations that analyze the ways in which language is used by organization members to generate fantasies, sagas, and stories that forge a collective vision.

One of the most common areas of language study in organizations is the analysis of narratives, described by Mumby (1987) as a primary symbolic form used to express organizational ideology. The narrative paradigm proposed by Fisher (1984, 1985) suggests that human beings possess the innate collective ability to create and share stories. Narratives are defined by Fisher (1984) as "symbolic action-words and/or deeds that have sequence and meaning for those who live, create, and interpret them" (p. 14). Fisher's definition suggests that both rituals and language would fall within the bounds of the narrative paradigm. Bormann's (1983) taxonomy of symbolic convergence delineates several key elements essential to the generation of group consciousness. In chaining "fantasy themes," organization members enact meaningful vicarious incidents that lead to "inside jokes" relating to previously shared fantasies. A "fantasy type" provides a recurring script within a group's culture. Collections of shared group fantasies blend to form "rhetorical visions" that serve to identify distinct cultures. The process of convergence culminates in the formation of "sagas" that embody organizational ideals. Bormann et al. (1982) describe a saga as a "collective memory" comprising the achievements and future visions of an entire organization.

A saga functions as one of the symbolic components of organizational cultures. Clark (1972) views the role of a saga as that of reconstructing organizational history in order to emphasize its origins and triumphs over adversity. Clark reconstructed "developmental histories" of small, cohesive college environments, including Reed, Antioch, and Swarthmore. He found that sagas were often introduced by the founder of the organization in order to illustrate, in story form, the core values and mission of the institution. Often, the saga details a unique accomplishment of the organization, such as a decision made by a key figure that ultimately helps the community triumph over adversity. Clark suggests that sagas, handed down through several generations, have positive effects on organizational participation and effectiveness and also provide a unifying function that links internal divisions among subcultures.

Throughout organizational culture literature, shared narratives are credited with the power to create cohesive and productive cultural communities. As we have seen, culture researchers frequently combine symbolic and systemic frames to illustrate the function of stories in facilitating commitment and in helping employees cope with ambivalent contexts. For example, Wilkins (1983b) gleaned organizational stories through employee interviews and then, by means of attitude scales, ascertained that commitment was higher in organizations where a larger number of stories were told. In these more committed organizations, story content tended to be more favorable in regard to policies and procedures of the company.

By using employee interviews and content analysis of employee publications, Martin et al. (1983) developed a typology of common stories that delineates two categories of settings: positive and negative. In the positive settings, administrators are perceived as competent, approachable, and tolerant of employee mistakes, while in negative organizational scenarios, administrators are viewed as incompetent, closed, and intolerant of errors. Martin et al. suggest that the stories reflect tensions arising from the conflict of individual versus organizational needs and values. Stories function as a way for employees to rationalize past errors and to either identify with a benevolent institution or to distance themselves from what they perceived as less desirable institutions.

As we have discussed, much of the contemporary literature on stories tends to draw away from interpretation and to focus on the function of stories within a particular context. For instance, Martin and Powers (1983) hypothesize that supporting a management philosophy statement with a story should increase commitment to that philosophy. They also suggest that stories will produce higher levels of commitment than other forms of information such as statistics. In addition, commitment tends to be higher in contexts where stories are congruent with management policy. Since organizational stories seem to have a decided impact on attitudes and cognitions, they will continue to assume a prominent place in functionalist and interpretive research.

In this section, we have focused on how shared symbolic artifacts, like rituals or narratives, serve to create and bind distinct communities. Interpretive approaches may be designed to let salient symbols emerge directly from the native point of view, rather than imposing a researcher's objectified scheme. Another way to look critically at symbols would be to focus on how organizational symbols impact on the formation of oppressive organizational structures or serve to constrain certain subgroups. Functionalist approaches reframe symbols as key variables that affect the maintenance of organizational systems by increasing commitment or facilitating group socialization.

The previous discussion has delineated three framing devices useful in an analysis of organizational culture: systemic, cognitive, and symbolic. As we have seen, frames may overlap, or they may be combined by organizational researchers to assess the effects, congruence, and significance of organizational culture. The use of combined perspectives allows researchers to obtain a more holistic view of organizational contexts. In addition, reframing an investigation from another perspective enables researchers to discover aspects of an organization's culture that may have been overlooked previously. So far, we have explored crucial theoretical and methodological considerations in defining a culture construct for organizational analysis. Since culture is a phenomenon that undergoes continual transformation, chapter 4 considers the evolution of organizational culture in the lifecycles of both individuals and collective contexts.

Chapter 4

INDIVIDUAL AND COLLECTIVE CULTURE CHANGE PROCESSES: SOCIALIZATION, IDENTIFICATION, EVOLUTION

*If organizations face increasingly turbulent environments,
one might well advocate not strong cultures, but flexible
cultures, where flexibility hinges on cultural diversity
rather than uniformity, and on looseness in the application
of cultural assumptions.*
—E. Schein

As dynamic organisms, both individuals and organizations experience cycles of growth and change. It is essential to consider the role of organizational culture in the dual processes of an individual employee's socialization and identification coupled with the organization's progressive evolution. The following discussion provides an overview of the stages in the socialization process in terms of learning a corporate culture. Although employees engage in officially sanctioned and structured programs of socialization, individuals are concurrently learning the values and norms that characterize a variety of organizational subcultures. Through the process of identification, individuals choose to align their personal values and goals with those of the organization. In order for employees and organizations to grow and flourish, there needs to be an optimum match between cultural assumptions, values/norms, and personal meaning. Such mutually beneficial matching of personal meaning with cultural dimensions releases "ego energy" that serves to enhance dynamic organizational transformation.

SOCIALIZATION AS THE MASTERY OF CULTURE

Socialization is defined by many theorists as a process by which people learn the fundamental parameters of their culture. While primary socialization takes place in childhood and involves the acquisition of general knowledge concerning norms and skills pertinent to basic societal roles, a secondary socialization process is enacted when an individual needs to acquire specific knowledge related to more specialized positions in the societal structure, such as a particular employee task in an organization (Berger & Luckmann 1966; Rosengren 1986). The type of socialization discussed in relation to organizational culture, that is, the acquisition of more specialized cultural knowledge essential for successful functioning in an employment context may be termed "secondary socialization." Van Maanen (1975) refers to this process as the way in which a person learns the values, norms, and required behaviors that permit participation as an organization member. Louis (1990) likens the mastery of workplace cultures to developing competence in a foreign language. In addition to individual employee competence, socialization also impacts on the organization as a whole. As Schein (1990) has suggested, the intensity of group learning is a key factor in cultural strength and consistency.

As a "culture-bearing milieux," an organization engages in a process of socialization to impart "meanings" to new members (Louis 1980). In describing organizational socialization, Hofstede et al. (1990) emphasizes that learning the cultural practices appropriate in a particular context is a key element in the process. Mastery of cultural norms comes about through observation of symbols, heroes, and rituals. Jablin (1982) uses the term *assimilation* in a similar manner when he speaks of a process by which organization members are absorbed into the culture of an organization. Similarly, Louis (1990) describes *acculturation* as the process by which new members come to appreciate organizational cultures.

The task of mastering cultural norms becomes increasingly challenging in situations where there is much novelty or open conflict among nested subcultures. In addition to learning officially sanctioned corporate norms, recruits must evaluate cultural differences across an entire organization. Some researchers stress that the quality and type of the socialization experience may mean the difference between an employee's success or failure in the organization. For example, Goodall, Wilson, and Waagen (1986) define organizational success as the transformation of an individual into a "properly socialized" employee role. Conversely, organizational failure is equivalent to an individual's refusal or lack of skill in acquisition of "cultural level" knowledge. Cultural "fit" requires knowledge on the part of the employee that facilitates successful participation in established organizational rituals.

Socialization is often regarded as "organizational learning," a process by which knowledge about "action-outcome" relationships is developed (Duncan & Weiss 1979). Two general models of learning based on "trauma" versus "success" interact to facilitate acquisition of cultural knowledge. According to Schein (1985), the need to reduce anxiety within the organizational context motivates some employees to learn relevant cultural knowledge. A "social trauma" approach operates on the principle of pain reduction, while a "success" learning model is grounded in reward. Employees showing mastery of certain cultural norms or practices would experience positive reinforcement within a success-oriented organizational context. Cultural learning is also fostered through interaction with groups of veteran peers and mentors. Louis (1990) noted that veteran peers facilitate the acculturation process by conveying information about local work group culture. However, mentors give recruits an appreciation of organization-wide cultural ideologies and historical perspectives.

Cultural Functions in Socialization Phases

Cultural schemata function throughout an employee's organizational tenure in a variety of ways. The most commonly identified functions of organizational culture include: conveying a sense of identity, facilitating generation of commitment, enhancing social system stability, serving as a sense-making device, and guiding organizational behavior (Smircich 1983a). Certain cultural functions may be more salient dependent upon the particular phase of employee socialization. For example, Buchanan (1974) delineates three distinct phases characterizing a career cycle: socialization, performance, and outcome. The initial socialization stage of one year or less is considered a "basic training" in which a new employee acquires essential cultural schemata. At this early point in an employee's career, culture serves to make sense of a foreign environment and to provide rules for appropriate behavior, thus alleviating initial anxiety. Similarly, Feldman's (1981) three-phase model cites major stages in employee socialization as: (1) acquisition of appropriate role behaviors, (2) development of work skills and abilities, and (3) adjustment to work group norms and values.

Following the initial acquisition of essential behaviors and skills required for survival in the work group and the organization, most individuals experience a "performance stage" around the second through the fourth year of employment (Buchanan 1974). In this phase, emphasis shifts from safety and security to concern with achievement and added responsibilities. Cultural schemata may function in the performance stage to foster a growing sense of identification with the organization and its mission. In this model, the final phase of a career cycle, the "outcome stage," begins during the fifth year of employment and encompasses most of an individual's career. At this stage, organizational attitudes have passed from a formative to a mature level. Among fully socialized employees, an organization's culture functions to facilitate commitment. In many contexts, cohesive unitary cultures, with high levels of commitment, tend to exhibit increased social system stability.

In order to investigate the way in which socialization relates to organizational culture, researchers frequently select contexts exhibiting strong unitary cultures. For instance, Cushman, King, and Smith (1988) analyzed IBM's socialization process in terms of values and rules inherent in the implementation and maintenance of a corporate culture. Core IBM values emphasize respect for the individual and development of employee potential. In this context, managerial effectiveness is fostered through strategies that promote two-way communication. In addition, IBM formally endorsed corporate citizenship by stressing obligations to customers, stockholders, and suppliers. The rigorous socialization program at IBM seeks to ensure adherence to the corporate culture through a continual monitoring of employees at each phase in the process. Initial selection of entry-level candidates favors those individuals who have predispositions toward core cultural values and norms. As in other contexts emphasizing group cohesion, IBM trainees are forced to endure humility-inducing experiences in early stages of their socialization. The hardy survivors are then subjected to in-the-trenches training. At IBM, the acculturation process does not culminate after employee orientation. Continual retraining procedures help to monitor the competence with which employees implement core cultural values in their particular job.

Some organizations utilize the symbolic components of the corporate culture as a learning device in orienting new members. For instance, Kreps (1983) notes the efficacy of "folklore" as a means of learning culture in the socialization process. In a field investigation at RCA, Kreps used interviews, written documents, and artifacts to isolate the major substantive categories representing "folklore" in this context. The research team examined the sense-making interpretations exhibited by organization members in regard to symbolic content of the culture. The salient symbols and interpretive meanings associated with the RCA culture that emerged in the study were presented to new members by means of a videotape shown at orientation sessions. This synthesized, mediated version of RCA's "symbolic field" assisted in providing new members with their first impression of the corporate culture but could also be used as a refresher course in cultural reinforcement for veterans of the organization. The orientation videotape served in sensitizing employees to the appropriate norms and values that would be more fully learned through social interaction in the weeks and months ahead.

Cognitive Processing and Strategies

Each phase of the socialization process is characterized by cognitive, sense-making processes utilized by individuals in order to interpret new environmental stimuli. In describing organizational learning, Argyris and Schon (1978) note that individuals gradually acquire images or maps of approved organizational expectations. These conceptual images are used to detect matches or mismatches between their behavior and organizational norms. In this process, individuals strive to achieve a merger between personal values and organizational norms. The cognitive maps acquired during socialization enable organization members to classify experiences, to interpret individual and group behavior, and to provide a general sense of orientation (Pettigrew 1979; Spradley 1972; Van Maanen & Barley 1985).

Likewise, Louis (1980) delineates a model of newcomers' cognitive coping processes in their initial encounters with an organization. As individuals enter an organization, they engage in a "detection" process that serves to weigh differences between expectations and actual experience. In order to interpret these differences or "surprises," newcomers filter information in a sense-making process. This process involves consideration of others' interpretive schemes, local interpretive schemes, predispositions, personal goals, and past experiences. Following this sense-making process, individuals select behavioral responses deemed appropriate to the context.

Shared cultural assumptions, then, facilitate organizational interaction by preventing constant reinterpretation of meanings. The selective perception aspect of cognitive cultural schemata not only helps to facilitate information integration, but also reduces the anxiety inherent in novel or unstable situations. For example, Steers (1977) proposes that goal clarity and goal agreement must be present to alleviate work anxiety. Also, in a field study of a decision and development corporation, Smircich (1985) notes that reactions to incongruent perceptions of organizational identity result in feelings of pressure, stress, and despair. These negative expressions are played out on an individual level by increased confusion and conflict about roles and job responsibilities. In the socialization process, shared learning reduces anxiety resulting from an inability to understand events unfolding in a single unit or across an entire organization.

Organization members may use the symbolic content of a culture in order to interpret and assimilate new information. For instance, Brown (1983) interviewed organization members in an effort to discover how storytelling is used as a sense-making device throughout the socialization process. The study reveals two types of narratives commonly used in organizational contexts—task-related and relational. Task-related stories convey specific information to upgrade employee job skills, while relational stories provide advice regarding superior and peer relationships. Brown posits that the stories fulfilled three functions: descriptive, energy controlling, and system maintaining.

Descriptive stories reveal details about organizational life, while energy controlling stories work to enhance motivation. System maintenance stories reinforce accepted belief and behavior patterns in order to promote organizational stability. As organization members progress through the socialization process, the content of the stories gradually becomes more closely associated with the values of the organizational culture. In the initial socialization phases of "entry" (zero to six weeks) and "encounter" (six weeks to five months), stories describing sequences of events (mainly task-related instructions) tend to be most common. In the later socialization phases of "role management" (six months to one year) and "stabilization" (one year and beyond), individuals begin to associate events with organizational values more consistently, and they also form conclusions based on cultural expectations.

In addition to stories, new organizational members also make use of "messages," or brief oral injunctions, to help process information of the work culture. In interviewing employees of a small company, Stohl (1986) found that members were readily able to recall one or more messages that had a lasting influence on their subsequent work lives. These "memorable" messages often prescribe rules of conduct, offer strategies for dealing with varied situations, or provide a unique way of resolving crises. The content of the messages usually embody cultural norms and promote attitudes and behavioral rules that foster maintenance of the social system. These messages remain memorable to employees even after long periods of time because they are usually delivered in equivocal or difficult situations by a source considered credible.

In summary, an organizational culture functions during the socialization process by serving as a sense-making device and by guiding organizational behavior. The optimum outcome of socialization is a culturally competent individual, that is, an organization member who has the context-specific information to operate in an appropriate manner and to fit in with organizational expectations and norms (Deetz 1982). According to Schein (1985), competence is enhanced through the gradual acquisition of cultural knowledge, which builds a group repertory of problem-solving skills, that can then be applied to numerous organizational challenges. The knowledge and acceptance of an organization's core cultural schemata by its employees provides them with both competence and a heightened sense of identity. However, it is not enough for employees to possess knowledge of cultural norms or even to attain competence through appropriate application of those norms. Rather, individuals will be challenged, eventually, to align their personal value systems with organizational standards. If the socialization process has been successful in the long term, employees may then begin to identify strongly with core cultural dimensions.

CULTURAL ALIGNMENT AS IDENTIFICATION

A discussion of the socialization process is incomplete without an understanding of how individuals learn cultural norms and choose to adopt core cultural values as their own. Kelman's (1958) scheme of *compliance, identification,* and *internalization* is helpful in understanding how an individual becomes socialized in a particular organizational culture. Individuals may comply with certain organizational expectations initially, because they hope to achieve favorable reactions and avoid censure. In an effort to establish a self-defining relationship with the group or total organization, however, individuals must go a step further and identify with the accepted cultural values. Finally, internalization, occurs when individuals accept influence, because certain ideas and actions are congruent with personal values. Organizations attempting to build strong cultural ideologies should aim for the goal of having employees not only comply and identify with cultural expectations, but also integrate the values of the organization with their own personal value systems.

The success of any socialization effort depends, to a great extent, on the willingness of the individuals to internalize core organizational values and ideals into their own cognitive schemata. Louis (1983) notes that participation in an organizational culture is a voluntary choice. In any organization, there exists a range of behaviors that indicate the extent to which an individual has accepted cultural dictates (Schein 1990; Van Maanen & Schein 1979). The organization's choice of socialization pattern affects the way in which a newcomer may adjust to the culture (Jones 1986). For instance, one type of response, "rebellion," is a rejection of all organizational values and norms by the recruit, while a "custodial orientation," fosters total conformity to norms and assumptions formally espoused by an organization. An optimal midpoint between these extremes, termed "creative individualism," encourages an acceptance of essential or pivotal organizational values and behaviors but tolerates the rejection of less relevant or peripheral values. This type of response is functional for an organization, because it permits the infusion of new ideas into the system while maintaining stability across organizational ranks. Additionally, creative individualism sanctions innovative behavior that may impact positively on overall organizational growth.

The phenomenon of organizational culture would be nonexistent if groups did not align with certain elements in the social environment. Cheney (1983b) describes identification as a "symbolic process" that underscores "basic tendencies in social relations" (p. 144). As we have noted, Kelman (1958) posits that identification occurs when an individual "accepts influence" because of the desire to establish a satisfying, "self-defining relationship with a person or group" (p. 53). For Kelman, identification is the precursor of "internalization," the process by which persons adopt behavior, because it is congruent with their value systems or is intrinsically rewarding. Some contemporary researchers delineate the components of the identification process as membership, loyalty, and similarity (Cheney 1983a; Patchen 1970).

According to Cheney (1986), the process of identification can be explained by the Burkeian concept of "consubstantiality." Burke

(1950) describes consubstantiality as perceived overlap between two individuals or between an individual and a group. This overlap or sharing of certain concepts provides a basis for common motives and collective action. Through the sharing of identities, individual motives grow into collective social values. Cheney claims that the study of "identity networks," or the way in which particular groups create collective identities, necessarily entails an examination of their shared symbols, ritual, and ideology. The overlap of individual identities into "networks" is facilitated through the collective sharing of an organizational culture.

The act of identification performs important functions within organizational contexts. For example, Cheney (1983a) suggests that identification facilitates processes of sense making, persuasion, and decision making. In addition to these functions, identification has been linked with higher motivation, job satisfaction, and performance in organizations. Using a triangulated methodology involving interviews, surveys, and observation in a corporate field setting, Cheney sought to determine how an individual's organizational identification influences on-the-job decision making. He found that if employees perceived organizational interests as directly related to their own interests involving work-related decisions, they were likely to identify with the organization. Higher quality decisions resulted from employee identification with organizational interests, as opposed to just individual needs.

In another study of identification in organizational contexts, Cheney (1983b) content analyzed corporate "house organs," official in-house publications of companies. Cheney isolated three dominant techniques used in the publications to promote identification with the organization: common ground, antithesis, and transcendent "we." In order to establish "common ground," leaders strive to convey the idea that the goals of the organization are also the goals of the individual. Identification through "antithesis" occurs when employees unite on behalf of the organization against a common enemy. For instance, an internal publication in a nuclear power plant, encouraged the mobilization of employees against individuals lobbying for the closing of plants, by reasoning that such closings would not only harm the overall organization, but also result in the loss of worker jobs. Another graphic illustration of banding together to overcome an external threat was the series of televised commercial spots depicting a horde of U.S. garment workers linking arms and joining in song to collectively celebrate "Made in America" goods. Spots designed to increase the identification of U.S. consumers with garment and auto workers have recently stepped up their use of nostalgic World War II imagery to promote "patriotic" unification against the invasion of foreign competitors.

Similarly, the "transcendent we" identification technique emphasizes the unity of organizational goals and members' interests by using collective personal pronouns in the oral and written communications to employees. For example, slogans like "we're working together for our future" attempt to unite employee and company in pursuit of a common goal. Coca-Cola spanned two generations in reproducing their original TV spot that showed a multicultural crowd perched on a hillside in order to "teach the world to sing"; the updated version included children and grandchildren of original participants. At the time of the Gulf War, numerous amateur and professional videos were hurriedly produced that depicted masses of cheering locals congregated on the village green, or superstars, gathered in recording studios, to serenade the troops in collective support for Desert Storm. All of these examples reflect unification techniques to foster identification with collective cultural visions.

Rather than focusing on specific identification strategies, some researchers choose to concentrate their investigations on the conditions essential for organizational identification. For example, Brown (1969) surveyed employees in branches of the Tennessee Valley Authority and found that, in order for identification to occur, employees should perceive that the organization provided adequate personal growth opportunities. Other required conditions for organizational identification included the employees' perception that they possessed some power in the situation and the absence of competing sources of identification. In his study of scientists, Lee (1971) noted that organizational identification is more likely to occur in situations exhibiting congruence between individual and management goals, paired with participation in decision making. These studies also stress that high levels of identification strengthen the organization as a whole with outcomes including: increased productivity, higher motivation, and greater overall job satisfaction.

Factors affecting levels of employee identification range from structural constraints to individual events. For instance, in a university-wide survey, Tompkins (1975) noted that the structure of an organization may stifle identification. These researchers found that the closer employees were to each other in terms of organizational stratification, the more likely they would identify with one another. While in their study of the socialization process of graduate students, Bullis and Bach (1986) reported that specific turning points caused fluctuation in identification levels. Using a retrospective interview technique, these researchers plotted identification levels over an eight month period. In this study, receiving informal recognition caused the greatest positive change in identification levels, while the decision to devote more time to outside interests, rather than to organizational concerns, brought about the greatest decline in identification levels.

The Role of Identification in Commitment

As we have seen, identification is a necessary process both in the creation of corporate cultures and in the maintenance of subcultural groups throughout the organization. Some researchers claim that identification with the goals and values of an organization is the process by which commitment occurs (Mowday Steers & Porter 1979; Reichers, 1985). Commitment is defined as the relative strength of an individual's identification with and involvement in a particular organization (Steers 1977). Three factors comprising commitment include: a strong belief in and acceptance of an organization's goals and values, a willingness to exert effort on behalf of the organization, and a strong desire to maintain membership in an organization. Buchanan (1974) summarizes these three components as identification, involvement, and loyalty. As we have discussed, identification occurs when members adopt the goals and values of an organization as their own, while the involvement component consists of the degree of psychological immersion in work roles. Commitment is enhanced by loyalty or a feeling of attachment to the organization.

Organizational research pertaining to identification and commitment reveals a degree of redundancy in the conceptualization and operationalization of the two constructs. According to Cheney and Tompkins (1987), identification and commitment appear frequently in organizational studies as ways of describing an individual's alignment with the organization. These researchers argue that the two concepts are distinct but interrelated. The identification process is conducted primarily through language and involves an employee's expression of the desire to choose alternatives that promote the perceived interests of the organization. Conversely, commitment downplays verbal manifestations and focuses more on an individual's act of remaining with the organization. In Cheney and Tompkins's estimation, identification is a process that underlies the substance of the individual/organizational relationship, while commitment is the form of the relationship. It may be useful in our discussion to regard identification as an individual's cognitive alignment with an organization's core cultural assumptions, while commitment represents the behavioral verification of loyalty, as evidenced by the act of linking one's career to an organization's cultural vision.

Often, researchers relate organizational commitment to the desire to remain with a firm. In a longitudinal study of managerial turnover, Porter, Crampton, and Smith (1976) reported a decline in commitment prior to leaving an organization. In a study of turnover among psychiatric technicians, Porter, et al. (1974) noted that organizational commitment was a better predictor of remaining with an organization than was job satisfaction. In his discussion of organizational alignment, Gorden (1984) examines three traditional orientations that enmesh to produce high organizational commitment: instrumental, affective, and moral. An instrumental orientation presupposes that the costs of employee efforts expended are equal to the rewards accrued. Affective orientation to commitment is based on the strength of employee sentiment toward the organization, while a moral orientation is centered around employee belief that the mission of the organization is ethical. Researchers need to examine more closely the specific orientations by which their employees build strong attachments to corporate or native-level organizational cultures. Determining if allegiance to particular cultural values or norms is driven primarily by instrumental, affective, or moral orientations, in a particular context, may assist leaders in articulating more meaningful collective visions.

The relationships among organizational identification, commitment, and culture have not been explored fully but represent a challenge for future investigations. Although popular treatments of culture readily equate cohesive ideologies with the presence of committed employees (Deal & Kennedy 1982; Peters & Waterman 1982), researchers have not empirically linked cultural dimensions with organizational identification. The process of identification, or the alignment of an individual with the organization's assumptions, values, and norms, may indeed facilitate commitment, a tangible decision to remain with the organization. Empirical measures of the two constructs tend to overlap in terms of dimensions relative to employee alignment with the organization. Both identification and commitment, however, remain important outcomes of acculturation processes in organizational socialization.

STAGES IN ORGANIZATIONAL LIFE CYCLES

Just as individuals advance through a series of socialization phases, entire corporate structures evolve through distinct stages. Some researchers use a biological system metaphor to conceptualize organizations in terms of their birth and transformation to maturity. However, others argue that the laws governing the evolution of biological systems are not identical to factors molding a social system. Organizations differ in function as well as in their response to environmental factors. Rather than exhibiting stages of maturation, organizations may evolve in cyclical fashion, in response to internal and external demands. As organizations change, so do cultural assumptions, values, norms, and artifacts. The introduction of a new set of artifacts or alterations in operational norms may represent ways in which managers attempt to induce organizational change. However, evolution of organizational life cycles is rooted in the deeper assumption levels of a culture, requiring more time to alter than the short-term adjustment of surface artifacts. This section examines several models of organizational change, from both the lifetime and cyclical perspectives, with an emphasis on the evolution of culture.

Lifetime Cultural Models

The human biological lifetime is a metaphor that is used frequently to conceptualize organizational growth and development. An example of a lifetime scheme applied to the functional evolution of an organization's culture is Schein's (1985) developmental approach: birth and early growth, organizational midlife, and organizational maturity. The birth and early growth stage is characterized by the domination of the founder. In this initial growth stage of organizational development, culture functions as a source of identity as the organization strives for integration and clarity. In early stages of developing cultures, the emphasis is placed on socialization to facilitate identification and win commitment. A variation of the birth and early growth stage is the "succession phase" that occurs in existing organizations when a new leader is appointed. During a succession phase, culture may become a battleground between conservatives and liberals, and the new leader is judged on the criteria of preservation or change of existing cultural elements.

The second stage of cultural evolution in organizations occurs at midlife, the time of expansion (Schein 1985). During a midlife stage, numerous subcultures may gain strength and influence in an effort to challenge collective unity. With the loss of core assumptions, identity crises may emerge throughout the organization. In the advanced stages, such as maturity, the organization has attained internal stability. In stable organizations with strong unitary cultures, assumptions, values, and norms may act as both a source of strength and unity and as a potential constraint on innovation. In Schein's estimation, if an organization's culture does not evolve with environmental demands, it may become destructive by preserving past glories, which are no longer relevant to present and future needs. If a mature culture preserves essential core assumptions while maintaining flexibility, then stagnation will be averted.

Cyclical Cultural Evolution

Some theorists argue that organizations evolve through "life cycles," rather than biological lifetimes. Rather than basing organizational evolution primarily on a time dimension, these theorists maintain that other factors account more accurately for cultural growth and change. For instance, Cameron and Whetten (1981) suggest several predictable transitions that reflect the evolution of an organization's culture. The first stage, termed "creativity and entrepreneurship," involves creating an ideology and gathering sufficient resources to provide for its enactment. The second stage, "collectivity," is characterized by the emergence of a sense of unity and mission. High commitment and cohesion tend to exist in this state. In the final transitional cycle, "formalization and control," structures, procedures, and policies have become institutionalized and may lead to reduced flexibility. Mintzberg (1983) summarizes the cyclical evolution of culture in a three-stage process: rooting of an ideology in a sense of mission, development of an ideology through traditions, and reinforcement of an ideology through identification.

By examining the histories of five organizations experiencing significant cultural change, Dyer (1985) developed a model of cultural evolution. The model is based on changes in value orientations over time, and it outlines conditions under which culture change is likely to occur. The initial stage involves a perceived crisis that serves to call into question the prevailing ideology and norms espoused by current leadership. In ensuing developmental stages, alternative leadership attempts to advance new approaches to crisis resolution by initiating change in the organization's culture. As the conflict of old versus new assumptions accelerates, a new cultural elite is established as emerging leaders are eventually credited with having a more desirable approach to facing organizational challenges. The new culture is sustained through the gradual acceptance of distinct symbols, beliefs, and structures. The cycle repeats itself when the prevailing pattern is once again challenged by an organziation-threatening crisis. Dyer notes that in addition to a leader's key role in culture change, organization members, through interaction, serve as "culture creators" by extending and adapting solutions to challenges.

As we have seen, cultures grow and change in response to internal and external forces. In complex organizations, different departments or operating units may need to sustain diverse cultural characteristics, depending on their function and needs. For instance, Atkinson (1990) suggests that cycles of cultural evolution can be classified by functions of power, role, task, or person. A *power* culture is typified by a web of insider influence, such as in a family-owned business. In a *role* culture, represented by a Greek Temple, the maintenance of bureaucratic structure and function is key to survival. In developing stages, organizations often rely on role cultures in order to establish functional specializations and create policy regarding procedures and rules.

Due to rapid environmental changes, many organizations are evolving toward *task* cultures, which create networks for rapid communication while anticipating and adapting to change. Japanese style management approaches, with an emphasis on "team" or "clan" orientations, foster *person* cultures, which evolve through collective determination of the organization's future. It is quite likely that, in complex organizations, varying degrees of power, role, task, and person cultural stages assume prominence throughout the evolution across life cycles. While one cultural pattern facilitates initial growth, the organization needs to maintain flexibility by allowing alternative styles to emerge, given contextual needs.

Flexibility plays a key role in allowing organizations to meet both internal and external challenges that occur throughout growth stages. According to Adizes (1988), an organization's life cycle is determined, not solely by number of years, but by its ability to take risks. Growing and "aging" organizations are distinguished by subtle orientational shifts that eventually grow to dominate the culture. For instance, an "aging" bureaucratic organization tends to place more emphasis on form and procedure than does an "adolescent" organization that is experiencing dynamic flux, and is more likely to stress function. Tichy (1980) suggests that organizations must make cyclical adjustments over time in adaptation to three ongoing dilemmas. Firstly, organizations need to resolve technical design problems so that their resources yield desired outcomes. Secondly, the organization must cope with political allocation, or an equitable and functional distribution of power and resources across ranks. Lastly, organizations need to determine the optimum ideological cultural mix that binds factions of the organization through sharing of salient beliefs. Tichy notes at any given point in an organization's growth, the amount of energy invested in cycle adjustments may vary according to internal needs and external demands.

Based on interviews with communication professionals in a broad range of companies, Kinkead and Winokur (1991) formulated several models representing stages in cultural development. Stage one describes newly formed companies that are dominantly controlled by the original founder, often a charismatic superstar. With greater delegation of responsibility, subordinates may begin to evolve distinct subcultures. In a stage two, tradition-based culture, policy makers define and actively maintain a corporate culture by means of sophisticated internal communication channels. Cultural multiplicity is encouraged in a stage three environment; a corporate credo and value statement instills unitary beliefs that coexist with local office cultures. In stage four, a limited number of fundamental ideals form the corporate culture and are then applied at every level of the organization.

Cyclical Modes to Balance Unity and Pluralism

Many large organizations, such as a universities, multinational corporations, or nonprofit institutions with broad scope, provide for both cohesion and diversification by designating a few core corporate values and then allowing departments or divisions to interpret the principles in terms of their distinct specialization. For instance, the concept of a 'quality revolution' originates in strategic planning at upper levels and is reinterpreted and applied by management in consideration of divisional needs. Regardless of rank or area of specialization, quality is a guiding concept that can be shared and implemented throughout the organization.

An example of an attempt to reinforce the primacy of quality to both employees and consumers, is the Anheuser Busch slogan, "Somebody still cares about quality." In addition to quality, other corporate values promulgated in employee literature include, innovation and achievement. Anheuser Busch's corporate policy links innovation to its founder, who developed the first national beer shipped in refrigerated railers. The company defines excellence as the process of building on a strong history of achievement that paves the way for future accomplishments. The value of "family" also assumes prominence in the Anheuser Busch corporate credo. Since the culture of the beer company was shaped originally by the influence of family ownership and control, contemporary corporate policy still stresses the analogy of family in its employee communication and community involvement. Internal communication utilizes family motifs to foster commitment, and to salve labor disputes. The company also sponsors a growing number of community relations programs, devoted to alcohol and environmental awareness, reflecting consumer pressure for greater social responsibility on the part of large corporations.

Similarly, Sara Lee Corporation provides its employees in diversified organizational divisions with a printed statement of "the principles that guide us," representing value dimensions of the unitary corporate culture. From early socialization stages to retirement, the document serves as evidence that certain core values cut across diverse organizational functions. The key themes of Sara Lee's formalized corporate culture are symbolically stressed in the graphics of the printed statement, by use of capital letters, when referring to the primacy of "service," and "customer" needs. The statement reflects several common themes promulgated in complex organizations attempting to create or maintain a coherent unitary culture.

> SERVICE...To deal with integrity, fairness, and responsibility toward all. Service to Customers, the company, and each other is our first concern.
> SAFETY...To always provide for the safety and well-being of each other, our first responsibility of Service.
> TEAMWORK...To support and encourage a company of mutually supportive teams, our foundation for Service.
> QUALITY...To constantly search for better ways to improve productivity and efficiency by focusing on quality.
> VALUE...To build our business by offering Customers better product value and Service than they expect.
> IMAGINATION...To tap the brilliance in every person by removing

barriers to pride in workmanship and by driving out fear.
LEADERSHIP...To be the best in everything we do.
UNITY...To operate as Customer-focused companies unified by
proven Guiding Principles.

This type of formalized corporate statement of values is especially useful in developmental stages of a unitary culture and in
multinational organizations characterized by cultural and departmental diversity. In contemporary, complex organizational structures,
diversified subcultural clusters may actually enhance efficiency; however, a statement of core unifying values assists in maintaining internal stability in the midst of rapidly changing external challenges.
Organizations need to walk a fine line between cultural stability,
which provides clarity and fosters identification, and an inflexibility
that stifles growth and change. As we close this discussion of evolutionary models, it is helpful to consider the dimension of stability versus instability as a way of interpreting patterns of organizational culture evolution.

Cyclical Change as Stability Versus Instability

As we have noted, organizations and their cultures are in continual
flux. In field investigations of an organization's culture, researchers,
like photographers, attempt to capture images depicting patterns of
growth and development that appear significant in a particular context. However, by the time the film is developed, the image that
appears may not accurately represent current aspects of the cultural
mix. Rather than searching for rigid stages or patterns, researchers
need to analyze where the organization's culture may be headed in
light of current cyclical trends.

Although it is difficult to freeze an organization in time and to
typecast its culture within a certain growth stage, the parameters of
stable and *unstable* provide useful dimensions in which to summarize
basic patterns of cultural evolution. Stable organizations are those
described by Schein (1985) as "mature" and by Cameron and Whetten
(1981) as "collective" or "formalized." In stable organizations, there is
evidence of consistent leadership and firmly institutionalized policies.
For instance, a bureaucratic "role" culture represents a form of structural stability. Although such organizations frequently exhibit clarity
regarding the organization's mission, the high degree of internal stability may potentially constrain innovation, if carried to an extreme.

On the other hand, most organizations need some measure of stability in order to achieve employee identification with a coherent vision and mission. When coherent corporate cultures manage to coexist successfully with clusters of diversity across the organization, then innovation becomes possible and the stable culture will grow and evolve.

Unstable contexts are representative of newly developing cultures where leadership has attempted massive transformation in structure and policy. Whether in a "founder" or "succession" stage, unstable cultures strive for integration and clarity, due to imposed changes of familiar artifacts, values, and norms. Unstable cultures may also result from a change in cultural cycle. For example, in order to adapt to externally imposed change, an organization might evolve from a familiar, role-dominated context into a task cycle, with increased demands for high activity and rapid communication. In order for organizations in flux to move toward greater stability, each individual within the unstable context needs to develop a sense of personal and collective empowerment in helping to shape the organization's future.

As this chapter has emphasized, organizations and their employees are never frozen in time at one evolutionary stage or cycle. Rather, the energy generated in the creation and maintenance of corporate cultures, engaged in dynamic interplay with native subcultures, creates cycles of stability and instability. Leaders need to monitor the cultural growth patterns within their organizations for patterns of stability and instability. Organizations that maintain an optimum balance between clarity regarding core cultural dimensions, coupled with the flexibility to welcome innovation at all levels, will not only survive but flourish. As we have seen in this discussion, the organization's leadership is a crucial element in socialization efforts and in the management of culture at any stage in an organization's life cycle. The next chapter will consider several key perspectives on how leaders function as culture creators, transformers, or managers.

Chapter 5

CULTURAL MANAGEMENT AND LEADERSHIP

Following and administering rules might have been dandy
in the placid environments of yesteryear. Not today.
Managers must create new worlds, destroy them, and then
create anew. Such brave acts of creation must begin with a
vision that not only inspires but encourages people to take
day-to-day risks involved in testing, adapting, and
extending the vision.
—T. Peters

Make your culture people-oriented. Recognize that
developing a culture in which people can thrive and grow
is the route to quality improvement. Flexibility, creativity,
and continuous improvement come from a culture where
people are treated as being more important than capital
and technology.
—P. Atkinson

In addition to assessing the scope and evolutionary patterns of
a corporate culture with its web of native subcultures, it becomes
important to explore the dual roles of leadership and management,
as a topics of concern for both researchers and practitioners.
Specifically, this chapter will discuss some of the current perspectives on leadership, culture, and change, as reflected in organizational literature. In the discussion, we will consider the challenge
facing contemporary organizational leaders in maintaining a balance between transactional versus transformational management
styles. Organizational culture change requires the ability on the
part of leaders to "reframe" their contexts in order to initiate the

process of cognitive and symbolic transformation. The theoretical concepts discussed in the first portion will provide a framework for a case study, presented in the chapter's conclusion, that illustrates the role of leadership in the collective generation of an organization's vision and mission.

Two contrasting logics appear in organizational literature when examining the structure of management: information and ideology (Cummings 1983). Dominant rational organizational paradigms have generated much research framed in a "management-by-information," approach, one that is logical and linear, emphasizing outcomes of control and efficiency. By contrast, much organizational culture research is framed in a "management-by-ideology" philosophy, characterized by a tendency to design management processes and organizational systems that serve the expressive functions of individuals and society. Both researchers and consultants who espouse an ideological focus on leadership consider the ways in which leaders can alter the symbolic elements of an organization through the management process.

A diversity of opinion exists, however, as to whether culture can, or should be, "managed." Martin, Sitkin, and Boehm (1985) suggest that opinions regarding this topic range on a continuum from a "pragmatist" to a "purist" perspective. On a practical level, many organizational consultants and managers engage actively in initiating strategic cultural interventions that are designed to enhance outcomes such as commitment, productivity, or employee satisfaction. On the opposite end of the continuum, purists assert that culture emerges and is, therefore, not amenable to direct control by any individual or organization (Morgan, 1986). Further, to foist a prepackaged corporate-initiated culture upon unsuspecting natives is unethical.

Ethical considerations involve the impact of workplace culture on the human character. For example, Deetz (1985) cautions prospective "culture managers" to consider the potential effects of planned innovations on the human beings within that context. In the critical view, conceptual systems need to be designed to enable full expression and representation of organizational constituencies. Likewise, Adams and Ingersoll (1985) stress the importance of examining critically, the "managerial metamyth," a pronounced bias toward rational and technical values like efficiency and predictability. Imposing corporate cultures that stress only rational values may function to alienate subcultural groups and discourage innovation. Deetz encourages managers about to become change agents, to engage in a "soul searching" process. In approaching planned innovations, managers need to discern "what kind of people we will become over time" if an idea or procedure is implemented in this context.

LEADERSHIP, CULTURE, AND CHANGE

When discussing the role of culture in an organization, an important distinction needs to be drawn between management and leadership. In discussing emerging megatrends for the next century, Naisbitt and Aburdene (1990) point out that the dominant principle of organization has shifted from management, in order to control an enterprise, to a leadership function, which serves to empower people and to assist the organization in adapting to change. This new style encourages self-management, autonomous teams, and entrepreneurial units. In this view, leaders and managers differ in orientation, mission, assumptions, behavior, and results. The control orientation of the manager enables the achievement of short-term goals that can be readily reported and assessed. A longer-term, leadership orientation strives for grasping larger relationships, is focused on renewal, and plans for change.

The creation and embedding of cultural assumptions pertains more to the function of leadership than that of management. An effective leader facilitates, rather than imposes, a vision that will inspire identification at every level of the organization. In addition, effective leaders create collective visions by empowering their own people through sharing power. A coherent vision, then, allows managers to maintain core cultural values by evaluating their daily strategies on the basis of how a particular action will help achieve the long-term vision. As Naisbitt and Aburdene (1990) suggest, emerging corporate heroes are increasingly those who shun traditional hierarchy and build highly profitable companies through vision, commitment, shared power, and responsibility.

The dual functions of leadership and management impact different levels of a culture. Leaders facilitate the shaping of the more abstract, enduring cultural assumptions through vision and mission statements. Cultural managers, on the other hand, seek to alter the more tangible, artifactual levels of culture, thereby creating or reinforcing more immediate behavioral norms. The shared value level of a culture evolves through the combined efforts of both leadership and management functions. Ideally, leaders, in collaboration with representative constituencies, will sculpt a vision that is brought into the realm of "everyday life" by managers, who elicit employee support in making the vision a reality through the achievement of tangible goals at every level of the organization. Current trends show leadership and management functions converging in a type of facilitator, who, through long-term vision and shared responsibility, maintains a delicate balance between flexibility and control.

The Cultural Question: To Transact or to Transform?

The difference between an ideological culturally-oriented management style in contrast to a system control-oriented style can be explained by analyzing organizational leadership according to two categories: transformers and transactors (Burns 1978; Atkinson 1990). Transformational leadership is characterized by adjectives such as *visionary*, *inspirational*, *intuitive*, and *creative*. Transformers keep their feet on the ground however, by maintaining an active and challenging approach to change. Rather than acting as visionaries, transactors function more as managers with a short-term orientation that is focused on people and the task at hand. Adjectives that describe the role of a transactor include *practical*, *concrete*, and *tangible*. The primary goal of transactional management is to maintain stability through clarification of processes and procedures.

If leaders do not distinguish between transactional and transformational styles, they may fall short of achieving the desired amount of culture change. For instance, Wilkins and Patterson (1985) suggest that one of the main reasons that corporate culture change initiatives fail is that interventions manage only surface, artifactual manifestations, rather than the deeper assumption level. If mangement attempts to impose unfamiliar values or norms from above, desired innovations may prove ineffective, because embedded assumptions remain unchanged. Fitzgerald (1988) concurs that culture change is much more complex than adjusting overt symbols; it involves, rather, a gradual alteration of core organizational dimensions. Similarly, Nord (1985) suggests that although culture as a management tool has the potential to become the subtle difference that results in organizational transformation, the desired change will occur not immediately but over a period of time.

Other erroneous views on the role of leadership in culture change include attempting to "buy" a prepackaged culture that has worked in other contexts or engaging in a "cultural revolution" that rapidly abolishes currently accepted norms with little consideration of the consequences. As Bettinger (1989) notes in observation of corporate mergers, a thorough understanding of existing cultures must precede any change efforts. Change that imposes "foreign" assumptions, norms, or values on a community without considering or even building on strongly held prior conceptualizations will not succeed. Rather than assuming a defensive stance regarding organizational change, Kissler (1991) counsels leaders to become proactive "change riders," rather than reactive change resisters. Leadership that refuses to be threatened by inevitable change can "harness" the power generated in change processes to ultimately strengthen the organization's culture.

Culture change involves a process by which transformational leaders alter the form and content of the organization's symbolic field. In order to do this, leaders engage in a threefold process of embedding, transmitting, and reinforcing cultural values and norms. Transformational leadership functions in helping to shape an employee's perception of an organization's culture. There is some evidence to suggest that leaders who provide guiding examples for employees tend to facilitate the learning of cultural norms through role modeling. For instance, Nair (1988) stresses the primacy of "personal example," before a "vision" statement is ever set on paper or discussed orally. Also, the process of symbolic leadership is enhanced through the power of metaphors in embedding and transmitting cultural norms and values. Since metaphors reach deeper cognitive and emotional levels, they provide a viable means through which leaders may frame new cultural assumptions and facilitate change (Berg 1985; Krefting & Frost 1985).

While transformational leaders engage in embedding and transmitting core assumptions of a corporate culture through vision and mission statements, the formal systems designed by transactional managers serve to reinforce cultural values and norms. Specifically, what managers attend to, measure, and actually control communicates relevant cultural information. Also, formal organizational policy governing recruitment, reward allocation, and retirement rituals either reinforces or negates the guiding vision and mission. Sathe (1985) suggests that managers consider several crucial areas when seeking to maintain a prevailing culture. Behavioral compliance to cultural norms is an essential first step in perpetuating a culture. However, behavioral compliance gained through an external reward system alone will seldom alter deeper levels of culture. Managers need to assist employees in acquiring justification for culturally linked behavior through intrinsic motivation. A collective vision that employees find appealing assists in providing justification for culture-based normative behavior. Also, the use of credible verbal and nonverbal communications that reinforce cultural values and norms serve a maintenance function for managers. Finally, Sathe notes that the hiring of those who "fit in" with the prevailing culture and the removal of cultural "deviants" completes the perpetuation cycle.

Rather than perpetuating the existing culture, managers seeking to facilitate culture change should plan their interventions at key points in the cycle of compliance, justification, and communications. For example, Siehl's (1985) field investigation of a microcomputer company provides evidence of a manager's ability to generate shared cultural orientations among employees. Siehl's study focuses on an assessment of employee values regarding the perceived importance and level of commitment both before and after a major company transition. The transition involved a new regional director who articulated a set of three values—productivity, professionalism, and responsibility—which he hoped to inculcate across employee ranks. Through interviews, Siehl found that employees rated the recently articulated values of productivity and professionalism as being very important, and, after eight months, greater behavioral compliance with innovations related to these value orientations was evident. It appeared from the study that although the regional director functioned as a "culture manager" in the initial articulation of the value dictates, much of the actual justification and acceptance process occurred over time within peer interactions.

In the opening discussion, we considered the necessity for leaders to attain an optimum blend of strategic organizational vision and managerial efficiency in order to facilitate culture change. One of the keys to initiating culture change is the leader's ability to "reframe" an organizational context. The process of reframing involves viewing complex organizations from a variety of perspectives and maintaining a flexible attitude toward change. Following a general discussion of the concept of 'reframing,' we will utilize "total quality management" and the "passion for excellence" approaches as examples of strategic attempts to induce value-level change in an organization's culture.

Reframing—The Key to Competent Cultural Leadership

Since culture change is often understood as a cognitive reframing process, it becomes crucial for leaders to develop a growing competence in their ability to select from a variety of frames to fit distinct organizational contexts. Bartunek (1988) defines reframing as the imposition of a qualitatively new template on a particular context. A different cognitive scheme may act as a "lens," allowing the viewer to observe a context from a totally novel angle. As we have discussed, exploring alternative images can create new ways of thinking about organizations (Morgan 1986). The advantage of using a framing perspective when discussing organizational leadership is that the concept can be generalized for a variety of contexts, from corporate to nonprofit. Bolman and Deal (1991) propose several frames that are useful in understanding leadership as a multifaceted endeavor. In a *structural frame*, the leader is a "social architect" who engages in the process of analysis and design of systems that will support desired outcomes. From a *human resource frame*, leaders are "servants" and "catalysts," providing for employee support and empowerment. On the other hand, leadership becomes advocacy and coalition building when viewed through a *political frame*.

Although the organization's culture is sculpted by use of structural, human resource, and political frames, the *symbolic frame* is likely the one most closely aligned with management of an overall vision. The symbolic leader plays the roles of "prophet and poet" in the creative process of defining and articulating an inspiring vision that will support the organization's mission. Also, one of the most challenging tasks of a symbolic leader is in mobilizing the ranks, in the collective generation of vision and mission statements. Corporate-level visions need to become shared in order for organizational identification to occur. In addition, if the vision and mission are not relevant to employee ranks, then cultural changes aimed at the overall organization will be futile. If changes in the corporate culture are promulgated without organization-wide participation and consent, then native subcultural groups may tend toward greater fragmentation from any unitary vision.

In articulating collective visions, symbolic leaders need to consider two essential dimensions—destination and path. In Nair's (1988) view, a path provides specific "roadmaps" that describe in tangible terms how to reach a destination, the desired end point. As we have mentioned, a symbolic vision should emerge from a leader's deep understanding of what people in the organization want; in this regard, it becomes futile for "outsiders" to craft an organization's unique vision. Symbolic framing should begin with a level of understanding on the part of leaders that includes a knowledge of the values held by the specific individuals and groups across the organization, as well a firm grasp of market realities and emerging trends. One way for leaders to develop this familiarity is to spend time with internal and external constituencies in a nonauthoritative atmosphere that fosters the free exchange of ideas, providing a basis for a shared corporate vision. If the organization's vision is not collective, there will be little alignment with unitary cultural elements. In Nair's estimation, if leaders succeed in winning over a "critical mass" who actively affirm the vision across the larger organization, then change efforts will move forward more efficiently.

A similar point of view regarding change and the reframing process is evident in Denison's (1990) culture and effectiveness model, which is based on the premise that current organizational norms are shaped by future vision. The model provides leaders with four criteria on which to measure organizational effectiveness: *adaptability, involvement, consistency,* and *mission*. The components of the model describe essential building blocks for leaders to construct coherent cultures. In stable cultures, a mission sets forth a public definition of the function and purpose of the organization. In addition, an effective organization will exhibit a high level of consistency regarding a shared, coherent system of beliefs, values, and symbols across organizational levels. Involvement, or a sense of ownership, as evidenced in high levels of employee identification, is also needed to create effective cultural contexts. However, strong unitary corporate cultures can degenerate into stagnation if leaders do not maintain an adaptability in relating with the external environment. Leadership in effective organizations provides for the monitoring of emergent issues shaping the larger society, assessing their impact, and adapting vision and mission in light of external demands. In summary, leaders striving for high levels of adaptability, involvement, consistency, and mission will succeed in giving life and structure to corporate visions.

In planning for culture change, then, leaders need to develop competence in reframing their complex organizational contexts from a variety of perspectives. While a symbolic frame enables transformational leaders to articulate a collective vision, the structural, human resource, and political frames also need to be recognized as the contexts through which cultural innovations are implemented. The next section will discuss the symbolic reframing of corporate cultures through articulation of visions grounded in quality and excellence.

SYMBOLIC LEADERSHIP IN QUESTS FOR QUALITY AND EXCELLENCE

In the last section, we spoke about the importance of considering the dual functions of transformational leadership and transactional management in articulating and implementing cultural assumptions, values, and norms. Working to build collective unitary cultures requires the adoption of goals that are relevant to every employee. In many organizations today, objectives grounded in achieving high levels of excellence and quality form the core dimensions of corporate culture. Atkinson's (1990) "seven S's" model provides a starting point for the ensuing discussion of the quality and excellence approaches, used widely in contemporary organizations. It has been traditional for most companies to give credence to the "hard S's" of strategy, structures, and systems when engaging in planning processes, defining roles by function, and providing the technological support to achieve prescribed outcomes. However, with an increased interest on the part of leaders to define their corporate culture, there is a growing awareness of the importance of the "soft S's," as crucial factors in the implementation of quality and excellence cultural orientations. These "soft S's" are more representative of elements that define distinctive contextual cultures: staff, skills, style, and shared values.

To initiate organization-wide programs of excellence and quality, it becomes essential to consider all "seven S's" for a holistic approach. However, Atkinson (1990) stresses that companies today need to acknowledge that organizational culture is the key to enacting change in the decade ahead. Relying on the traditional "hard S's" alone provides a mechanistic solution to a human problem. This philosophy is grounded in the idea that you need first a passion for change and then the systems to make corporate vision a reality. The following discussion centers around how leadership and management can function jointly to initiate change in organizational cultures through the implementation of quality and excellence value orientations.

Questing for Quality

Total Quality Management (TQM) is a strategic approach to producing the best product and service possible through constant innovation. The TQM approach gained steam in the 1980's, due to increasing competition from Japan and the establishment of public citations, such as the Malcolm Baldrige National Quality Award, established by Congress in 1987. Rather than citing specific products or services, the Baldrige award recognizes quality awareness and achievement in three categories within the private sector: large manufacturers, large service companies, and small businesses. Although the TQM approach began as a corporate initiative, it actually points to a growing realization on the part of leadership, whether in the private or public sector, that quality is an organization-wide problem. Current estimates attribute that within industry, close to 80 per cent of quality problems originate in areas other than manufacturing. For example, Atkinson (1990) asserts that a concern for quality should be shared equally across divisional boundaries, whether it be in management, financial accounting, personnel, or sales, because TQM has an impact on "everybody, everywhere in the organization." And across organizational boundaries, a heightened awareness of quality can also be found in social service agencies, universities, or arts institutions, as well as in multinational corporations. The TQM approach reflects the "passion for excellence" movement that stresses the need to create and maintain cultural values/norms that support functional systems designed to ensure quality.

In his "Ten Commitments of Leadership," Atkinson (1990) sets forth an agenda of basic principles necessary for transformational leaders to successfully launch and implement organization-wide visions of quality:

- Search for challenging opportunities to change, grow, innovate, improve.
- Experiment, take risks, and learn from mistakes.
- Envision an uplifting and ennobling future.
- Enlist others in a common vision by appealing to their values, interests, hopes, and dreams.
- Foster collaboration by promoting cooperative goals and building trust.
- Strengthen others by sharing information and power, increasing their visibility.
- Set an example for others by behaving in ways that are consistent with your stated values.
- Plan small wins that promote consistent progress and build commitment.
- Recognize individual contributions to the success of every project.
-Celebrate team accomplishments regularly.

Questing for Excellence

The principles of Atkinson's (1990) quality agenda are typical of organizational initiatives designed to maintain an ongoing "passion for
excellence." Implementation of corporate cultures grounded in excellence often require leaders to espouse a philosophy oriented toward
radical cultural reform. Rather than "being" excellent, the emphasis is
more on "doing," with an understanding that excellent firms need to
rapidly adapt and evolve. The primary role of the leader in this high
energy, frenetic environment is that of a change agent. In his "thriving
on chaos" philosophy, Peters (1988) urges leaders to be "obsessed"
with creating an environment that fosters constant innovation. Leaders
are directed to dissect their "old corporate world" and build a radical
new one grounded in a love of change. In order to implement this
change-oriented leadership style, organizations are encouraged initially to conduct an "excellence audit," designed to assess level of agreement regarding five critical areas across the organization (Harris &
DuMond 1990). These critical areas include: customer responsiveness,
innovation, people empowerment, love of change, and creation of new
systems to meet the needs of a world in flux.

The first step in the use of the audit is to have upper-level
management select representative value statements that best
describe the organization's orientation to the five critical areas. In
addition, CEOs and strategic planners identify "bold goals" that
define the "vision" of the organization. According to Peters (1988),
effective vision statements are inspiring, clear, and challenging. The
organization's vision describes desirable outcomes and serves as a
stabilizing force in a chaotic world. In addition, the vision needs to
be crafted, so that employees are empowered at all stages of their
career. The primacy of the organization's most important constituency, whether it be consumer, public, or target audience, also
assumes utmost importance in vision statements. Once a vision is
articulated at upper organizational levels, the next step involves
defining the organization's "strategic distinction." In other words,
what makes this particular organziation unique among competitors?
Discovering the unique role of the organization in responding to the
needs of employees and primary external constituents is another
crucial area to consider. Peters advises companies striving to forge a
distinctive organizational vision to compare their "bold goals" with
statements about what makes their organization unique.

Unlike corporate credos that are handed down with little input from those in the trenches, who will need to live the vision daily, this vision statement is designed to be tested. Criteria suggested by Peters (1988) for testing a vision include the idea that the statement should be broad enough to encourage challenging goal statements and innovative adaptations up and down the organization. Also, the vision needs to encourage risk taking and failures that will result, ultimately, in a better product or process. The failure of hierarchies to solve problems, along with the dilemma of information overload, has given birth to a network style of management. The creation of networks requires a shift from vertical to horizontal communication flow. Lateral and horizontal linkages that cross divisions and enable more bottom-up communication will assist leaders in acquiring the information they need to prescribe strategy. In addition, networks empower the individual and deemphasize destructive competition while fostering cooperative ventures.

"Real-World" Case Quests

There is a growing body of cases documenting the successful implementation of network-oriented styles that serve to maintain cultures grounded in quality or excellence. The use of more "team" approaches reconfigures the management function as that of a "coach," "teacher," or "facilitator." In recent national press coverage, a Xerox manager of corporate quality, explained to reporters that the traditional management stance of "telling and controlling" doesn't lend itself to creating "an environment of empowerment." Xerox's much touted "team" focus includes annual surveys of management practices that ask workers to rate their superiors in twenty-seven categories of performance. Survey results are discussed by managers and staff in feedback sessions where they collaborate on a plan to improve problem areas. At the managerial level, an increased focus on listening to employees is also evident. In another interview with business analysts, Linda Miller, an assistant plant manager at Ford Motor Company, claimed that maintaining strong relations with the twenty-two hundred engine assembly workers is the most important part of her position. As the highest ranking woman in the Ford manufacturing hierarchy nationwide, Miller spends at least one hour daily walking through the plant, talking and listening to employee concerns. According to Miller, if workers feel they are doing a good job and that they are a part of the company's future, then enhanced product quality will result.

Another technique that some large companies are using to make sure that information travels upward is the formation of councils composed of employees representing different levels and business units. A recent feature in the business press cited the fact that, the CEO of Manville Corporation meets regularly with his President's Council, a group of diverse employees who are charged with alerting him to communication problems at any level of the hierarchy. Since the council's inception three years ago, Manville has developed a set of governing principles and has encouraged supervisors to promote more effective horizontal communication by actively involving their staff in the extension and application of the corporate directives. Instead of taking orchestrated plant tours, the president and other top officials favor informal, drop-in visits with workers. These more informal, spontaneous ventures of superiors into the "trenches," reflect the popular, "management by walking around" philosophy, which deems it dangerous to spend more time in one's office than out among constituents. In addition to increased oral communication, Manville's president sends letters describing the company's strategic goals to employees at their homes; the letters always include a return envelope for comments and critiques, which are then answered personally. In addition, the president sends monthly voice mail messages to employees and invites them to respond using the same system.

As we have noted, a transformational leadership style focuses on people and communication processes as much as on results. Greater information sharing builds the trust that will lead directly to commitment, not just compliance. Using a George Bush motif, John F. Welch, Jr., the chairman of GE, describes his vision to shareholders as a "kinder, gentler workplace where front-line employees are as important as top-level managers." Whether dubbed "collaborative management," "team work," or "commitment-based management," the goal remains the raising of productivity through shared decision making. Likewise, James A. Perdue, son of Frank Perdue, the chicken magnate, says that he is "reforging" the family poultry company by decentralizing power to give workers greater voice in making their jobs safer and more efficient. The evolution of the Perdue leadership style becomes evident in juxtaposing two generations. The image of "father" Perdue as "a tough man, who made tender chickens," was well known to TV viewers of the last decade. Current CEO, "son" Jim, describes himself as "a tender man," who works to distinguish his style from that of his father's by "loosening the reigns on managers and workers alike" (see News Coverage Citations in References).

These corporate examples of quality and excellence cultural orientations reveal a trend in leadership today as a movement from a short-term endeavor, based on self-interest and personal advancement, to an evolving process that considers the long-term impact of contextual values, norms, and, decisions on individuals and organizations. The principles in corporate agendas for quality and excellence provide a summary of several contemporary trends in literature on cultural leadership and managment. One emerging trend that is changing the shape of corporate cultures is an increasing focus on participatory democracy. For instance, Naisbitt (1982) notes that organizations are working toward increasing the level of involvement for their internal and external constituencies, as evidenced by increased shareholder activism, consumerism, and inclusion of outside board members. Enhanced concern for employee rights and empowerment are all indicators of increased organizational participation. Externally, corporations are engaging in more active participation in political and social arenas.

As the prior discussion has shown, if a corporate vision is not collectively generated and shared, identification will seldom occur and managerial innovations designed to alter cultural artifacts, norms, and values will have very little effect. Many contemporary organizations are responding to a call for corporate responsibility and the empowerment of employees through shared decision making. Ethical leaders craft organizational visions and missions that become collectively shared, because they build on employee voice that spans all levels of the corporate ladder. In his forecasting of social trends, Naisbitt (1982) claims that organizations will experience change when there is a confluence of fluctuating values and economic necessity. These factors call for reconceptualization of current perceptions and resulting goals. In order to be effective, however, the process of reconceptualization must be a continual one. Strategic planning may well prove worthless, unless there is initially a strategic vision. The vision provides a clear image of what the organization wants to become, while the mission specifies logical pathways for pursuing relevant goals. The distinct cultural value orientations within an organizational context function as a catalyst in merging reality with vision.

As we have seen, the quest for excellence and quality has crossed both private and public sectors in initiating organizational transformation through culture change. One particular organizational context that appears to be engaged in the process of reconfiguring vision and mission, in light of changing internal and external demands, is the contemporary arts institution. The following case investigation of a history museum traces the evolution of a collective vision and mission over the course of three decades. Specifically, the case examines the role of leadership in three cultural growth stages: founder domination, institutionalized control, and collective revisioning.

EVOLUTION OF A COLLECTIVE VISION AND MISSION

As we have discussed, transformational leaders strive to articulate shared visions that carve out an organization's direction in a changing environment. The evolution of corporate culture in the context of a museum provides an interesting case study of the role of leadership in change processes. Over the last decade, nonprofit institutions across the country have experienced massive restructuring in administrative ranks. Paradoxically, cuts in federal and state funding seem to be having a longer-term, strengthening effect by forcing arts organizations to become more sophisticated about marketing and generating new revenue sources via the corporate sector. According to social forecasters, the decade of the nineties will witness revolutionary shifts in leisure time priorities, with the arts gradually replacing sports as society's primary pastime (Naisbitt & Aburdene 1990). Fortuitously, arts organizations are gearing up for the onslaught of heightened interest. In particular, museums are reaching out to a more general public with blockbuster exhibits that pander to popular taste. The unstable nature of the emerging strategic corporate cultures within arts organizations makes this an ideal context in which to observe both the evolutionary stages and the leadership functions discussed in the last two chapters.

The museum context that will be discussed in this brief recap of a case investigation, is the Strong Museum in Rochester, New York This particular history museum provides a fitting context for constructing a timeline of evolutionary stages in its cultural development, because the institution has recently engaged in the process of collectively generating vision and mission statements. Also, the three-decade lifespan of the museum enabled the examination of leadership styles at several different stages. A variety of data-gathering methods were used to chart evolutionary stages of growth. First, a series of interviews with the CEO, president, and key staff members provided a variety of perspectives on both the history of the organization and the recent strategic planning initiative. Secondly, a critical textual analysis of museum print materials, including promotional brochures and annual reports randomly selected across the organization's history, served to generate key cultural themes communicated to internal and external constituencies. Finally, the analysis of documents used in the strategic planning process was helpful in charting the future direction of the organization.

Growth Stage One: Founder Domination

Frequently, organizational culture investigations begin with focusing on the founder as an enduring force shaping underlying assumptions and values. The Strong Museum in Rochester, New York, began as the dream of Margaret Woodbury Strong, a wealthy socialite who found her identity in being, first and foremost, a collector. Through her extensive travels, Strong acquired a very large and eclectic grouping of objects that became a "museum of fascination" displayed in her large home. In 1968, Strong made the first move toward institutionalizing her "collecting hobby," as she was granted a museum charter from the New York State Board of Regents that established a corporation "for charitable, educational, and public purposes." By the time of her death the following year, Strong had amassed half a million objects, including twenty-seven thousand dolls, ninety thousand bookplates, and an extensive display of Japanese artifacts and miniatures.

Strong left her estate to the museum corporation with a perpetual endowment and gave executors free reign to transform "a static personal collection into a dynamic professional museum." In the decade that followed after the death of the founder, a team of professionals was enlisted to provide both the "intellectual meaning" and the physical control necessary for the general public to appreciate an overwhelming and diversified collection. It was in this institutionalization stage that the museum's culture evolved from being defined primarily by the personality of the founder, to being a more formal, mission-driven organization.

Growth Stage Two: Institutionalized Control

The evolution of the museum's culture from founder stage to a management controlled institutionalization stage occurred in the 1970s as an early mission to govern the vast collection was articulated. Under the leadership of its first director, Holman J. Swinney, the museum's purpose was described as that of "providing a comprehensive portrayal of American society and culture." Swinney was instrumental in formulating an early mission for the museum by moving the collection beyond the "static possessions of a single individual" to positioning the institution as engaged in "an ongoing effort to enhance our appreciation of the past, and supplement our understanding of the present." In this early institutionalization stage, the museum directors focused on the managerial task of gaining control of the diverse collection, as it was relocated from the private residence of the founder to a public site of contemporary architectural design.

As more formal managerial control moved the museum toward institutionalization, the initial mission served to clarify its identity for internal and external constituencies. The developing mission explained the purpose of the museum as that of collecting, preserving, exhibiting, and interpreting popular materials owned and used by Americans during the era of industrialization. Taken together, the artifacts explored the historical, social, and cultural fabric of American life in the Northeast between 1820 and 1940. Planners reasoned that the ordinary objects acquired and displayed by Americans reflected cultural ideals that the country as a whole emulated in any particular era. The highly specific nature of the early mission assisted in achieving the goal of controlling an overwhelmingly diverse collection of seemingly unrelated objects. The nomenclature devised for classifying cultural objects grew into a universal system that earned the museum a national reputation among historians and curators even before its formal opening.

As the museum opened to the public in the early 1980s, its formal mission was more clearly perceived nationally than on the local scene. For Rochesterians, the Margaret Woodbury Strong Museum was popularly regarded as the personal collection of its "somewhat eccentric" foundress. In this post-founder stage, museum management had purposely attempted to reflect some of the personal style and values of the foundress in the newly opened, modern structure. For example, a display housed in a room adjacent to the museum's entrance chronicled the life and "dream" of Margaret Strong. Also, a large portion of the second level was devoted entirely to Strong's personal collections. As Siehl (1985) found in analyzing organizations in post-founder stages, leaders have a better chance of implementing innovations if they first build upon and reinforce the existing symbolic content and adjunct value systems. The museum's management appeared to be maintaining institutional equilibrium by perpetuating that link between the past and the present.

Growth Stage Three: Collective Revisioning.

In the late 1980s a new CEO moved the museum to a third stage of cultural development—creation of a shared vision. President G. Rollie Adams led the museum through a fourteen-month program designed to collectively generate not only a revised mission, but a guiding vision for the museum, as it moved into the next decade. The endeavor began with the appointment of a Long-Range Planning Committee, consisting of seven trustees and six senior staff, including department heads and vice presidents. Committee members engaged in extensive "issue identification" sessions in order to generate both existing and desirable cultural assumptions regarding the mission of the museum. Research was conducted in order to provide the data that would fuel the "issue sessions." A combination of focus groups, surveys, and interview techniques were utilized to gather information regarding perceptions about the museum from staff, volunteers, the general community, and specific constituencies, such as educators.

As we have noted in the chapter discussion, transformational leadership facilitates a process whereby core organizational values are revealed in order to provide a firm foundation upon which to build successful management. For example, Francis and Woodcock (1990) advise leaders to facilitate the "unblocking" of organizational values through use of appropriate survey research techniques. In this process of "unblocking," symbolic leaders may isolate clusters of values that will assist the organization in achieving its goals. A similar procedure was implemented at Strong Museum, as facilitators led three sessions with the full board and thirty staff representatives in order to share information, surface and test assumptions and generate issues. Then, eleven planning committee sessions reviewed findings, developed a vision and mission statement, and drafted future goals. Task forces, composed of a board member and up to seven staff members, then developed strategies to carry out the mission through goal setting. In addition, department managers facilitated extension of the vision statement by engaging their "teams" in writing goals and strategies relevant to their own unique function within the organizational scheme.

The result of this extensive process was the adoption of the museum's first strategic plan. In preparing a vision paper setting forth the plan, Adams, president and CEO, refers to the museum as being "at the crossroads to its future" with "major challenges ahead." Built into the plan is a strategy that calls for developing an annual review process to keep it "evergreen." In addition to annual review, the "evergreen process" mandates that the museum form a new planning committee and undertake an entirely fresh planning effort at least every five years. The original planning document also includes an appendix detailing the major challenges ahead, with recommendations for confronting the emerging issues. For analytic purposes, the collectively generated "vision," and "mission" statements are quoted from the strategic planning document:

VISION STATEMENT

The Strong Museum is the leading history museum in the country. It provides the highest quality service to the public through its superb collections, and through educational programs that are innovative, interactive, imaginative, and entertaining.

These programs are achieved through sound research and scholarship, and an aggressive acquisitions program. Active and balanced participation by board, staff, volunteers, and the community assures the museum's success. The museum attracts and generates all the financial resources it needs. It enjoys a clear identity as the best museum of everyday life in America.

MISSION STATEMENT

The Strong Museum is a public educational institution that collects, preserves, and interprets historic artifacts, manuscripts, and other materials that tell the story of everyday life in America after 1920, especially in the Northeast during the era of industrialization. The museum uses these materials as the basis for exhibitions, publications, educational programs, and other activities that educate, enlighten, provide enjoyment, and connect the past to the present for diverse audiences.

The museum provides these services consistent with the highest standards of museum practices, scholarship, and management, including appropriate application of technology and effective generation and use of financial assets.

As we have seen, the extensive process of creating a new shared vision for Strong Museum involved every level of the organizational structure. The role of leadership as facilitator in shaping a collective vision is a key element in the process. However, the idea of managing cultural artifacts is also evident in some of the more visible changes at the museum that rapidly followed the adoption of the strategic plan. For example, a name and logo change signalled an official distancing from early founder-dominated and institutionalization stages. Previously, the memory of the foundress served to shape the image of the institution in the name, the Margaret Woodbury Strong Museum. The shortened name, Strong Museum, both conveys a more powerful, memorable identity, and opens up new avenues of pursuit for the institution that are consistent with its future vision. In addition, the museum's old logo displayed the full name of the foundress, and the major color promotional brochure depicted Margaret's famed doll collection, reinforcing the local image that the museum was mainly for "doll enthusiasts." The new logo, which was selected after extensive design audits and focus group testing, displays the initials S. M. in flowing script, and the cover of the brochure shows a wide range of objects with potential appeal both for devotees of popular culture and nostalgia buffs.

Other obvious artifactual innovations include a revitalized lobby with colorful banners, large-scale graphics, new signage, more plants, and increased seating. The renovated lobby sets a festive tone and creates a more effective visual impression of the museum's mission. All of these artifactual changes show an enhanced awareness on the part of the museum that the communicative power of design is primary in creating a corporate identity and reinforcing cultural change (Olins 1989). The new name, logo, and visual imagery enhanced the efforts of the museum's public relations and marketing divisions, which were striving to assure that the image of Strong Museum would accurately reflect its mission to external constituencies.

The museum's new tag line, "Exploring American Life," is also reflective of several major cultural shifts that are evident in the institution's first strategic plan. First, there was a decided effort to extend the collections beyond themselves, to reveal a broader social significance and richer levels of meaning. This process began with the elimination of 1940 as an end date in the museum's collecting period and mission. The prior museum mission, which was set forth in the institutionalization phase, grew out of limitations imposed by the scope of the founder's personal collection and reflected social issues generated in the age of industrialization. The new mission brought the museum into the information age, and allowed historians to consider emerging trends shaping the late twentieth century. Rather than focusing on the curiosity factor of static objects, the museum now seeks to integrate contemporary issues, in order to define the significance of exhibits. For example, one of the current exhibits that reflects the expanded scope of the mission deals with "altered states" and assesses the social significance of alcohol and drugs in American life.

A second major accomplishment resulting from the expanded vision and mission was the museum's outreach to new audiences through enhanced community relations. The public program, Summer SUN (for Strong's Urban Neighborhood), was planned and developed in cooperation with the staffs of three Rochester community centers. The month-long program introduces the museum to African-American and Hispanic children, ages six to twelve, through the use of music, crafts, and artifacts. Also, the museum sponsors an annual Advanced Placement Conference, where local high school students join with leading area college and university faculty to explore various topics of American history falling within the museum's mission.

Consistent with the new mission and the tag line, "Exploring American Life," exhibits have become more reflective of racial and eth-nic diversity by probing social issues of significance to minority groups. For example, a recent exhibit displayed cartoons and caricatures depict-ing destructive stereotypes of Irish-American immigrants, drawn when they struggled to find a place in the melting pot. Also, the Anti-Defamation League of B'nai B'rith joined with the museum's public affairs and educational staffs to present programs in conjunction with the exhibit "Jewish Life in America: Fulfilling the American Dream. The recently mounted exhibit, "Neither Rich nor Poor: Searching for the American Middle Class," focuses on the values, rather than the econom-ic issues, that define this segment of society. Other exhibits explore uni-versal issues that cut across societal barriers. For instance, "Memory and Mourning," an exhibit in the final planning stages, will trace the history of dealing with death and the grief process.

Expansion toward more entertaining, interactive displays with wide popular appeal enabled the museum to draw more than a hun-dred thousand visitors in each of three consecutive years. Exhibits like "Ice Cream for All," funded by the Eskimo Pie Corporation, traced the history of product packaging and marketing, as well as the social function of ice cream in American life. Under the auspices of the extended mission, the museum is mounting more exhibits that reflect trends in popular culture. Examples include interactive exhibits, like "Selling the Goods: Origins of American Advertising" and "Radio Daze: The Radio in American Family Life," that consider the impact of electronic and print media on society.

The pattern of cultural evolution at the museum has shown a continual expansion of scope in aligning with other constituencies. One of the goals included in the strategic plan speaks about pursuing a more proactive leadership role among museums and related institutions, locally and nationally, through collaborative programming. Opening the grounds for local families to celebrate Fourth of July or to spend a "New Year's Early Eve" at the museum has led to clarification of Strong's image among local groups. Increased community involvement is also evident in the launching of a Corporate Partners' Program, designed to increase the level of funding from the private sector.

The current cultural state of the museum is typical of the high activity atmosphere of an "unstable" growth culture that is striving to merge objectives with the larger vision. G. Rollie Adams, the president and CEO, speaks frequently about the "feverish pace" of public programming and promotion, as staff scramble to "market the museum and its programs aggressively." From Adams's standpoint, he views the staff as "stretched to the max," with the future only promising "more of the same." Grounded in its collective vision, it seems probable that the museum's culture will evolve into a more stable stage, but one that avoids stagnation by "evergreening" its vision, mission and strategic goals on a regular basis.

The case study described in this section attempts to provide some insight into the cycles of leadership that emerged in the creation and maintenance of a corporate culture. An overview of cultural evolution at Strong Museum reveals a progression from a highly individualized culture dominated by the personal preferences of the founder to a more public, control-oriented institutionalization phase, marked by a relatively narrow mission. The present stage of the museum's corporate culture reflects an attempt to go beyond institutional management to a more visionary leadership stance, as is evidenced in the collective generation of an organizational vision. By involving representatives from all organizational constituencies, both internal and external, the museum strategic planners engaged in the challenging process of allowing cultural assumptions to surface and to project into a future where contextual reality aligns with strategic vision.

PART II

Chapter 6

AN EMPIRICAL EXPLORATION OF
CULTURAL DIMENSIONS

*If culture is to survive its fashionable wave and turn into a
useful and meaningful concept both for organizational
researchers and for practitioners, it is necessary to spend
more effort on empirical research, rather than on debating
opinions.*
—S. Sackmann

As the models discussed in part 1 have illustrated, organizational culture is a multilevel phenomenon that represents the shared,
symbolically constructed assumptions, values, and artifacts of a particular context. In addition to having multiple levels, many
researchers affirm that workplace cultures also exhibit multiple
dimensions that, in some cases, prove to be generalizable across organizations. The shared value orientations that compose a distinct culture are symbolically negotiated and evolve over time across organizational ranks. The process of cultural evolution in organizations can
be observed both in individual employees and in life cycle patterns of
the system. Through socialization, individuals learn to comply with
cultural expectations, and may choose to identify with and internalize
core cultural assumptions. As organizations evolve, their functional
uses of culture differ. For instance, an organization in an early growth
stage may find certain dimensions of culture more useful in binding
its members to core unitary assumptions than would an organization
in more mature developmental stages. Finally, an organization's lead-

ers assume dual roles in regard to culture. Transformational leadership facilitates the articulation of a collective vision, while a transactional mode enables the management of structural and functional aspects of norms or artifacts.

This brief overview of some of the key elements stressed in part 1 leads into the theme that contemporary researchers frame organizational culture from a variety of theoretical perspectives and examine their contexts from diverse methodological perspectives. As noted in the epigraph at the beginning of this chapter, the debate regarding an optimum approach can distract us from the real issue at hand—construct development. According to Reichers and Schneider (1990), the "paucity" of empirical research on organizational culture is preventing the necessary synthesis and critique that would result in advancing the construct past definitional debates. With this goal in mind, the case investigation presented in the next two chapters aims to illustrate the efficacy of a multiconceptual and multimethodological approach to organizational culture that may prove useful in a variety of contexts. A complex organization that represents a particularly challenging cultural context to assess is that of the large urban university. The next section presents a rationale for the use of a university in an analysis of organizational culture by providing a brief overview of pertinent research in this context.

ORGANIZATIONAL CULTURE IN THE ACADEMIC CONTEXT

Although much of the contemporary culture research tends to focus on corporate organizations, another viable context for the study of organizational culture is that of higher education. Brucker (1985) notes that the guiding principles of excellently managed corporations tend to be similar to many mission statements found in academic contexts. Brucker compares Peters and Waterman's (1982) guiding principles of corporate excellence to the academic context and notes several similarities. These similar corporate and academic standards include respect for the power of ideas and for the worth of individuals in the organization. Also, Brucker cites other common university standards of excellence as the realization that success cannot be achieved by short-term results, the belief that individuals and institutions act on their environment, and a recognition of the importance of collective activity. As higher education seemed to lose a strong sense of its collective identity in the 1960s, with the emphasis of many universities on short-term goals, such as increasing enrollment and expanding structural resources, faculties were drawn away from identification with the institution and allied themselves instead with gaining prestige in a particular discipline. The strategic plans of many contemporary universities, however, reveal a push for excellence through more cohesive unitary cultures. In order to achieve greater unification, Brucker recommended the creation of university communities that promote the collective vision and mission of the institution across ranks and that work to deemphasize departmental affiliations.

Many educational institutions today are experiencing internal instability, because they must confront issues of the economy and public trust. According to Phair (1992), educators are no longer perceived as "secure in their ivory towers" but are facing similar crises as the rest of society. The "two-headed monster of shrunken budgets and adverse publicity" (Fry 1992) has resulted in academia's newfound vulnerability. Although corporations have battled a lack of public trust for two decades, some analysts see higher education as the last major American institution to "fall from grace." With accountability and solvency as two vital problems to tackle, public universities are struggling to reach external constituencies with the message that their organizations are being managed in an ethical, cost-effective manner. In their battle to regain public confidence for their organizations, many corporate CEOs have espoused a transformational leadership style that fosters clarification of vision and mission for internal and external constituencies. So, too, there is a growing trend among university administrators to emerge from their ivy halls, in order to collectively negotiate and clarify organizational vision and mission.

Although universities and corporations are jointly confronting issues related to the economy and public trust, academic organizations do differ from profit firms in their primary mission and goals. Based on a traditional, three-pronged mission of research, teaching, and service, universities do not have a simple "bottom-line" measurement of success. In a classic study, the Carnegie Commission on Higher Education (1973) drew attention to several essential themes governing the mission of academic institutions. One of the core themes is that campus environments should be conducive to the intellectual, aesthetic, ethical, and skills development of individual students.

In addition to empowering individuals, another essential task of a university is to provide a critical voice to bring about needed societal renewal and reform, rather than to endorse the passive maintenance of the status quo. The primary "product" produced by a university, that of an expanded mind or an enriched psyche, does not lend itself to traditional corporate standards of bottom line measurement. Concern for preserving freedom of expression at universities also gives rise to ethical questions surrounding the imposition of corporate-level cultural values that may inhibit critique of administrative policies. However, if university leaders strive to facilitate the development of cultural visions that are collectively negotiated, and that allow for differentiation at all organizational levels, then academic contexts will be enriched.

Universities As Organizational Cultures

Interestingly enough, the goals stated almost two decades ago by the Carnegie Commission—and found today in many mission statements of universities—are closely allied with contemporary recommendations for productive organizational cultures. For instance, the traditional emphasis on individual initiative and freedom of expression in academic contexts reflects the fostering of an "entrepreneurial" spirit in organizational ranks. In an academic context, the researcher who discovers a new way of looking at a problem not only benefits an individual discipline, but also enriches the organization. The organizational structure of a university, with its emphasis on autonomous units such as classrooms and departments, reflects a contemporary corporate trend toward decentralization. This structural autonomy encourages localized adaptations and provides room for self-determination. As Weick (1976) has noted, "loosely coupled" systems, like universities, often encourage greater diversity in strategies for solving problems, and they may also have the ability to adapt to a wider range of environmental changes. In Weick's estimation, the structure and resulting mission of a university may afford a type of "cultural insurance" that facilitates adaptation in times of radical change. The quest for excellence in both corporate and academic contexts involves a delicate balance of individual empowerment and identification with a collective vision.

So far, we have viewed organizational culture in universities through a systemic analytic frame, by focusing on the structural and functional aspects of academic cultural contexts. Other researchers select academe as a valid context for cognitive cultural investigations, because universities are organizational structures composed of individuals engaged in the collective enactment of meaning systems. For instance, Treadwell (1987) cluster analyzed statements made by members of a college community about organizational "image." He isolated several "image" dimensions unique to the academic context in the case study, such as friendship, service, mission, reputation, excellence, and individual development. Treadwell found greater agreement on abstract, rather than pragmatic views of the organizational image.

Likewise, Tierney (1988) developed a framework to diagnose cognitive cultural dimensions in collegiate institutions. Specific dimensions isolated in the investigation include: environment, mission, socialization, information, strategy, and leadership. Another study that attempted to assess coorientation on dimensions of culture in an academic context is Harris and Cronen's (1979) rules-based analysis of a social science department. Four constructs were elicited from the scholars surveyed: scientific/historical, community/backbiting, power/powerlessness, and service/substance. These cognitive investigations conducted in academic contexts reveal similar organizational dimensions as those isolated in some corporate cultural analyses.

In addition to overlaying systemic and cognitive frames, an assessment of university culture can also be approached by analyzing symbolic stories that reconstruct an institution's history. For example, Clark (1972) interpreted shared cultural assumptions in the sagas, or "developmental histories," of three private liberal arts colleges. In each instance, Clark notes that the development of sagas over time increased loyalty to the organization and decreased personnel turnover. In order for sagas to gain hold in academic contexts, several conditions seemed essential. First, senior faculty must become key believers, committed to the practice or lesson illustrated by the saga. Second, rituals should reinforce the key values inherent in the saga. Third, alumni need to engage in perpetuation of the saga; and lastly, the student subculture must integrate the key ideas of "believing" administrators and faculty. Such symbolic approaches reveal how a university's cultural legacy is negotiated by natives through the process of symbolic interaction.

So far in this discussion, we have seen that researchers have used systemic, cognitive, and symbolic frames for their investigations of universities as viable contexts in which to assess organizational culture. In a systemic frame, researchers may conduct audits that reveal the unitary or pluralistic structural patterning of subcultures, across the ranks of a loosely coupled university. Also, cognitive congruence is an important topic for investigators seeking the core cultural

dimensions that shape university contexts. Finally, symbolic significance within a university context is frequently assessed by interpretation of sagas, which serve to create distinctive identities and foster
collective convergence.

Since the selected context for the case study of university
organizational culture that is described in this chapter is an urban
environment, a brief comment on the mission and practices of
institutions in urban centers is appropriate. Two decades ago, The
Carnegie Commission on Higher Education (1972) set forth several unique obligations inherent in the missions of urban institutions. The report stated that the term *urban university* implies an
obligation to respond to the educational and social needs of the
surrounding community. In addition, faculty research should necessarily be focused on contemporary problems involving the quality of life in the city. The "distinct urban mission" of universities
may also involve training for new occupations related to the
needs of the city and for providing cultural and recreational facili-
ties for local residents.

The Carnegie Report (1972) also discussed two opposing
themes, voiced by administrators and faculty, which revealed a
dichotomy in articulating a vision and mission for an urban university. One theme stressed the importance of closing the gap between
the campus and the city, while the opposing attitude encouraged an
aloofness to the needs of the city, in order to preserve academic freedom and autonomy. Two decades later, with the realities of a reces-
sion, many urban universities are seeking major roles in revitalizing
the economy by creating corporate, community, and university partnerships. For instance, a spokesperson for Pennsylvania State
University commented recently on the necessity for institutions of
higher education to become "agents for economic revitalization" by
"moving ideas out of the laboratory, and into the marketplace."
Universities in large urban centers need to articulate the amount of
interface with the community that proves most conducive to the
accomplishment of their overall academic vision and mission.

As we have seen in this review of investigations in academic
contexts, a number of researchers have noted the efficacy of studying
the university as an organizational culture. Few of these studies, however, have attempted to assess the psychological, sociological, and
historical range of cultural dimensions by using a measure based on
the previously discussed universal dimensions of culture: human
nature, the environment, time, activity, and relationships. The multi-

level organizational structure of the university community, with its shared ideological mission and distinctive symbolic artifacts, provides a viable context for an assessment of organizational culture. The following sections will provide specific detail on a field investigation that explores the range of cultural dimensions inherent in urban university contexts.

THE PROBLEM: ASSESSING RANGE OF CULTURAL DIMENSIONS

The problem forming the basis of this study is to create a viable method to assess the range of cultural dimensions in an organization over time and across structural levels. The methodology used in this study attempts to accomplish this goal by discriminating between two types of cultures, *stable* and *unstable,* and then assessing the psychological, sociological, and historical penetration of cultural dimensions within these distinct contexts.

The first step in the proposed analysis is to employ a type of known-groups technique to be able to discriminate between two cultures. As noted, this study examines organizations at two "known" stages of cultural development: stable and unstable. Drawing from descriptions of cultural cycles discussed earlier in the book, a *stable* stage of cultural development is one in which an organization has maintained consistent leadership over time and exhibits firmly established institutionalized policies and procedures. Schein (1985) termed stabilized stages of culture as "midlife" and "maturity," while Cameron and Whetten (1981) referred to a "collectivity" state, characterized by a sense of unity and mission coupled with high levels of commitment and cohesion. An *unstable* stage of cultural development is conceptualized in this study as an organization that has recently undergone major restructuring of administrative ranks and has instituted many new policies and procedures.

The overall purpose of this field investigation, then, is to discriminate between stable and unstable contexts by focusing on differences regarding perception of cultural dimensions and in varying levels of organizational identification. If stable and unstable cultures are distinct entities, they should differ in terms of the penetration of salient unitary cultural dimensions and also on identification levels. Stable cultures are more likely to exhibit high levels of collective agreement on core unitary cultural dimensions with less fragmentation throughout organizational ranks. The lack of cohesion regarding salient cultural dimensions in unstable cultural contexts may result in less clarity regarding a unitary vision, coupled with marked differentiation across organizational levels. Given these characteristics, the stable cultural context may facilitate the process of identification with the organization. As Lee (1971) suggests, organizational identification is more likely to occur in situations where there exists congruence of individual and management goals. Also, Mintzberg (1983) posits that strong ideologies are reinforced through identification. It would seem, then, that in stable organizational contexts, we might find dual outcomes of higher identification levels, and greater agreement regarding collective vision.

There may also be differences in the employees of stable and unstable cultures, according to their hierarchical placement and career stage. For instance, individuals at the top of the organizational ladder that are actively involved in strategic planning or in management positions requiring the enforcement of organizational rules frequently tend to agree more strongly with the officially "sanctioned" culture and may also exhibit higher levels of identification. In universities, members of administrative teams who are actively involved in strategic planning endeavors may tend to have a stronger attachment to the organization than some staff personnel, who perceive a lack of power in determining the fate of the university. Faculty often possess stronger departmental or professional affiliations, thus decreasing identification with a particular university.

Since the socialization process is designed to facilitate the penetration of cultural constructs throughout the organization, length of service should affect perception of core cultural dimensions and level of organizational identification (Hall, Schneider & Nygren 1970). A useful model used in this study to segment employee groups is Buchanan's (1974) career stages of socialization (one year), performance (two to four years), and outcome (five years and more). Because the three stages describe a gradual development of organizational attitudes, there is some likelihood that employees may differ in their perception of cultural dimensions and levels of identification over the three career stages.

So far, this discussion has focused on perceptual differences regarding salient cultural dimensions and organizational identification among employees at various career stages and hierarchical positions. In this study, these differences are explored by assessing the psychological and sociological range of organizational culture in stable and unstable contexts. In addition, historical cultural penetration, or the stability of salient cultural constructs over time, is another aspect that is crucial for researchers to consider. One commonly used method of tracking an organization over time is to study artifacts produced by that particular culture. Because stable cultures should exhibit greater consistency in salient constructs over time, the symbols produced by stable cultures may reflect this trend. Therefore, stable and unstable cultures should differ over time in terms of their print communications regarding cultural dimensions. Now that we have discussed a general overview of several key concepts that will provide the focus for this investigation, we turn to the selection of specific university contexts that will serve as models of stable and unstable organizational cultures.

Selecting Field Locations by Cultural Stability

This field study was conducted in two organizations of similar type, demographic characteristics, and function, yet with differing stages of cultural development (i.e., stable and unstable). The use of intact organizations with known characteristics for field research is a type of known-groups technique. The usefulness of known-groups technique in this study is that it enables the selection of organizations with cultures in both stable and unstable stages. *Unstable organizational cultures* are defined, for the purpose of this study, as institutions that have recently undergone major administrative changes resulting in massive structural and functional alterations across the entire organization. Often, in an unstable "succession" phase (Schein 1985), new leaders are forced to "ride out" a stage of turbulence, where they are judged negatively because they have not preserved salient cultural elements.

As we have discussed, the second cultural growth stage in this study is termed stable. *Stable organizational cultures* are characterized by an enduring mission, evidenced in strategic planning that is mounted by a consistent cadre of administrative personnel. In organizations with stable or mature corporate cultures, the majority of policies and procedures across subsystems have prevailed over time, so as to become institutionalized. Stability, in the form of a strong unitary culture, emerges from the penetration of salient dimensions through the ranks of the organization. Employees are aware of a stabilizing vision and the primary mission and goals of the organization in mature cultures. Because of their clarity and cohesiveness, stable cultures may also exhibit high levels of organizational identification.

The specific organizations selected for this study are two large urban universities in the northeastern region of the United States. One university meets the previously discussed criteria for unstable organizational cultures, while the other meets designated criteria for stable organizational cultures. At the time of the investigation, University A's (unstable culture) president had assumed office three years ago and had appointed a new administrative team to revamp many long-standing procedures throughout organizational subsystems. From its inception, the new administrative team in University A had initiated major upheavals in personnel structure and policy. In addition, the president was attempting to launch a major shift in the university's primary mission. Traditionally, University A preserved a strong localized flavor with an emphasis on community service. At the time of the study, it was perceived by many of the natives that the new president was attempting to refocus the university's mission to that of attaining a national reputation solely through athletic excellence. As we will discuss in depth later, this move on the part of the president resulted in perceptions across the ranks, particularly among senior faculty, that academics had taken a back seat to athletic prowess.

By way of contrast, University B (stable culture) had a president who held office for six years, a time period now considered longer than average in contemporary academic institutions. Although the president in the stable institution had intensified an ongoing thrust to enhance the national reputation of the university, he had also maintained the research mission that has consistently characterized the university for several decades. Although University B was noted for its innovative research, organizational changes in personnel structure and function initiated by the president and administrative team in the stable culture were not massive within the time frame of the study. In addition, the president was keenly aware of the organization's history and recent direction, because he had served on the administrative team of University B for a number of years prior to appointment.

Even though the selected universities exhibit differences according to cultural life cycle and mission, they do possess demographic similarities. For example, both institutions have enrollments of at least twenty-five thousand students and are located in urban centers that have recently experienced a transition from blue-collar-dependent economies to emergent white-collar, high-tech economic bases. Similarly, both universities have been in existence since the mid-to-late nineteenth century as private or city-affiliated colleges, and both institutions became state universities in the early 1960s. The two universities experienced major campus renovations in the past decade and are considered comprehensive research institutions. Although the effort appeared to be more intensive in the unstable context, both presidents had attempted to upgrade the athletic program at their institutions. Finally, each of the presidents had recently articulated ambitious five-year strategic plans designed to enhance or gain a national reputation.

METHODOLOGICAL PHASES

The research design of this study employed triangulation, the use of multiple methodologies or data sources (Denzin 1978; Jick 1979). A growing number of social scientific researchers strongly advocate triangulation as a way of more accurately assessing culture in complex organizations. For example, Smircich (1983c) describes triangulation as the merger of "etic" and "emic" perspectives that results in a more holistic view of social phenomena. Often in triangulated methodologies both quantitative and qualitative measures are combined in order to serve as internal validity checks throughout the study. The multiple methodologies utilized in this study were sequenced in three phases and included interviews, self-report surveys, and content analysis.

The three methodological phases in this investigation were designed to assess the psychological, sociological, and historical range of cultural dimensions within stable and unstable contexts. Phase one consisted of interviews with administrators to elicit key cultural dimensions found in both stable and unstable cultures. Building on interview data, phase two included a self-report survey, assessing agreement on core "corporate" cultural dimensions and determining the level of organizational identification. Analysis of survey results yielded the extent of collective agreement on core cultural dimensions and identification levels across structured tiers in the organization (administration, faculty, and staff) and within employee career stages (socialization, performance, and outcome). Finally, phase three of the methodology measured the stability of cultural dimensions over time, by use of a content analysis of print records. If the reader desires a more detailed explanation of the specific hypotheses tested in this investigation, the chart found in appendix A delineates the independent and dependent variables involved in research phases two and three.

Phase One: Interviews

The purpose of the interview phase of this study was to surface core cultural assumptions, values, and norms from the viewpoint of natives. Since an important aspect of the investigation involved discovering the range of core dimensions associated with the corporate, or officially articulated, culture found in the strategic plans of each organization, interviews were conducted with individuals occupying upper-level administrative posts in each university. As might be expected, the institution representing the unstable culture had more new administrators who had assumed their posts one or two years ago with the advent of the new administration. Out of the seven administrators interviewed at the unstable institution (A), only three had been with the university more than twenty years. By contrast, at the stable institution (B), five of the six administrators interviewed had been affiliated with the university for more than nineteen years.

The interview schedule found in appendix B was designed to pursue broad themes related to the previously designated "universal" dimensions of culture: human nature, environment, time, activity, and relational orientation (Kluckhohn & Stodtbeck 1961). For example, the value orientations of "good" versus "evil" human nature dimension were approached in the question "Do you think most employees here put in a good day's work?" Another example of a question probing human nature was "Do you have in printed form, any employee guidelines regarding rights or ethics?"

Two interview questions exploring the time dimension of "past" versus "future" included "Who could best tell the university's story, both presently and past?" and "To what extent is the university tradition-minded?" The "universal" themes derived from theoretical dimensions provided a workable framework for open-ended interview questions, which facilitated the gathering of a broad range of perceptions regarding salient values and norms operant in each university context.

The semi-structured, open-ended interviews (Goetz &

LeCompte 1984) were completed over a two-month span. Each administrator signed a form granting audiotape permission and the average length of an interview was one hour. At the completion of the thirteen interviews, the researcher listened to each interview and recorded statements directly pertaining to the dimensions of culture previously discussed: human nature, environment, time, activity, and relational orientation. A total of 240 statements were extracted from the interviews and recorded on index cards. Appendix C contains a coding scheme, based on "universal" cultural dimensions, which was used in both phase one, to sort interview statements, and in phase three, for the content analysis coding procedure.

Initially, the usable interview statements were sorted into five cultural dimension coding categories, with contextual-specific statements grouped into a sixth category, termed "culture/mission" because these statements pertained to the collective sharing of the threefold university mission of research, community service, and teaching. Examples of statements exemplifying shared context-specific "cultural" mission perspectives were: "the university is like a big family" and "as a public university, we have the obligation to develop the economic base of the local community." Secondly, the categorized interview statements were placed in one of two value orientations for cultural dimensions, as indicated in the coding scheme, and were analyzed as to their potential as survey items. Survey item selection proceeded by identifying representative, mutually exclusive statements for the evaluative ranges designated for each of the five cultural dimension categories. The next section will provide more detail regarding the survey instrument that was created from phase one interviews.

Phase Two: Survey

The second phase of the methodology consisted of a self-report mail survey sent to employees at the stable and unstable institutions. The two instruments used in the survey phase were the *Organizational Dimensions Survey (ODS)*, which provided a measure of cultural dimension perception, and a shortened version of the *Organizational Identification Questionnaire (OIQ)* (Cheney 1983a), which served as a measure for the dependent variable of identification. The forty-item ODS consisted of thirty statements, representing a range of theoretically derived cultural dimensions and the contextual "culture/mission" category (see appendix D, "ODS

Items in Cultural Dimension Categories"). Because the statements selected for the survey were originally quotes obtained from administrators during the interview process, it was necessary to make some minor wording changes for clarity in preparing statements for the final survey form. Also, several statements were rewritten in order to achieve a positive/negative wording balance in survey items. Respondents were asked to read each statement and indicate their level of agreement by selecting one of five alternatives: strongly agree (5), agree (4), neither agree nor disagree (3), disagree (2), or strongly disagree (1).

A second assessment instrument used in phase two of this investigation was the *Organizational Identification Questionnaire* OIQ (Cheney 1983a), which provided a measure for the dependent variable of identification. The OIQ has proven to be consistently reliable in past research. For instance, in a triangulated corporate field investigation, Cheney reported a Cronbach (1951) alpha reliability of .95, and a single-factor solution accounted for 86 percent of the total variance. Because of the unidimensional nature of the twenty-five-item OIQ, Cheney suggested that the measure may be used successfully in a shortened form. In their investigation of socialization among graduate students, Bullis and Bach (1986) reported a reliability of .90 using a seventeen-item scale. In addition, Miller et al. (1990) reported that their factor analytic investigation of the OIQ revealed unidimensionality over four time periods, but only twelve items contribute in a meaningful manner to the identification construct. The shortened version of the OIQ constitutes an affective measure of commitment, or the extent to which employees maintain a mutually beneficial relationship with the organization.

Because a shortened version of the OIQ had proven to be reliable, it seemed advantageous in this mail survey to use a limited number of items to maximize response rates. The fifteen-items selected for this study reflect three components of identification: similarity, pride, and emotional attachment (see appendix E, "OIQ Items in Components of Identification Categories"). The items represent a conceptualization of identification as an affective process that is the precursor of commitment (Cheney & Tompkins 1987). The mail survey sent to participants contained fifteen OIQ items and forty ODS items, randomly positioned on the final survey instrument.

Using the university directory as a sampling frame, respondents from each institution were selected by systematic random sampling.

Cohen's (1977) statistical power tables were used to determine adequate sample size. Because mail surveys yield low response rates and a 50 percent return rate was needed for adequate analysis (Babbie 1973), 400 respondents per university (total N = 800) were selected for the sample. The final rate of return for the survey was 54.5 percent for University A (n = 218) and 58.3 percent for University B (n = 233), yielding a total N of 452 respondents (56.5 percent).

Phase Three: Content Analysis

The third component of the methodology consisted of a content analysis of major university publications issued during a designated time period that were analyzed in order to assess historical penetration of cultural dimensions. For purposes of consistency, the time frame selected for analysis was the same six years for both institutions. The selected time period encompassed the entire tenure of the president at the stable institution. In the unstable context, the same six-year time frame proved useful, because it included both the initial years of the new president's service as well as the last three years of his predecessor. The coding scheme representing the five theoretical cultural dimensions: human nature, environment, time, activity, and relational orientation (see appendix C) was used for coding selected print materials in the content analysis phase.

The method of sampling utilized in this phase was based on Holsti's (1969) multistage sampling model. First, a type of publication was selected from the universe, then particular issues were chosen, and, finally, specific stories were isolated for analysis. Selected publications were university-wide vehicles of general interest, including the student newspaper, the faculty/staff newsletter, and the alumni publication. Both universities published comparable print vehicles of these types. Since the investigation focused on the core cultural dimensions representing perceptions of the university's "officially sanctioned" culture, the selected print materials aptly conveyed information portraying the "corporate image" released for the consumption of specialized constituencies.

In keeping with the second phase of Holsti's (1969) multistage sampling for content analysis, particular issues of the publication were selected by random sampling methods. Archivists at each university provided the researcher with a list of fall, spring, and summer publications within the six-year-long time periods. Each issue was assigned a number, and a table of random numbers was used to select particular issues. After the individual issues were selected, the third step in the multistage sampling was to make appropriate article selection from the issues. Articles selected for coding purposes were those in which the topic or theme pertained to some aspect of the overall university function or mission. Types of articles not included in the selection were those having limited university appeal, such as features on individual faculty personalities or news pertaining to one department. Story selection proceeded according to prominence in the issue, which was determined by headline size, column space, and page placement. Each issue yielded an average of two usable stories. A total of 208 stories met the criteria for selection. Once the stories were selected, each was photocopied and assigned a number and time frame category (years one to six).

Coding Procedures. Articles were assigned five codes, each corresponding to one of the value ranges for the five cultural dimensions: human nature, environment, time, activity, and relational orientation. A code of NA or (not applicable) was assigned to articles not exhibiting any characteristics of that cultural dimension. Coders read each article in its entirety and assigned an appropriate code for each of the cultural dimension categories. Specific coding instructions with a description of value orientation ranges for each category are described in appendix C. Two coders independently coded a sample of articles from each university, and the observed overall percentage of agreement for all five coding categories was .93. Using Scott's (1955) pi formula, an index of intercoder reliability for each coding category was computed. For categories one to three (human nature, environment, and time) the reliability was .90. Category four (activity) had an intercoder reliability of .89, and category five (relational orientation) had an intercoder reliability of .88. Discrepancies were resolved through discussion.

In order to clarify the coding procedure, examples from coded articles illustrating cultural dimension categories will be discussed briefly in this section (see appendix C for coding scheme and instructions). The first coding category, the *organization's orientation toward human nature*, contained three coding options: *good, variable,* and *evil.* A *good* human nature statement praised the achievements of individuals or groups. The following quote from an article on the investiture ceremony of the new university president illustrates a good human nature orientation: "If I had to choose the one factor that has impressed me most about the University, it would be our faculty." Later in the speech at the investiture ceremony, the president praised other groups of employees of the university: "An important strength of this institution is its first-class cadre of administrators and staff. These people are exceptionally loyal, hard-working, intelligent, and thoroughly professional."

The *variable* code was assigned to content within articles that acknowledged variability regarding human nature. For instance, one article described the establishment of a "secret visitor" program to check randomly on the appropriate behavior of staff personnel in the enactment of their daily duties. Another article coded in this category announced more stringent faculty evaluation procedures to be used in undergraduate courses. A human nature *evil* code was assigned to statements stressing the need to restrain or limit the power or responsibility of individuals, due to their own innate ignorance, apathy or lack of skill. Due to the positive public relations thrust of university publications, such as the alumni magazine, the evil category was found infrequently. One example of the human nature evil orientation, however, was a statement in an article from a university student newspaper: "The state government does not trust the University's Board of Trustees, Chancellor, or campus Presidents with even the most elementary decisions concerning the institution's welfare."

The second cultural dimension coding category, the *organization's orientation to the environment*, contained three codes: *subjugation*, *harmony*, and *control*. The environmental *subjugation* code was assigned to statements describing how external constituencies prevented the organization from achieving its potential. Examples of this category included a quote from a university vice president who spoke of the "stranglehold of rules and regulations imposed by a constraining, controlling state bureaucracy." Another quote exemplifying the subjugation coding category described the university's frustration at being treated like "any other state agency," causing the state to "run its universities like its prisons."

Another coding option within the environment dimension was *harmony* or how the organization promoted mutually satisfying relationships with outside constituencies. An example of this orientation was found in a quote from one of the president's addresses in which he encouraged faculty and staff to make the local residents "feel as though they are a part of our extended academic community." The final coding category within the environment cultural dimension was *control* portraying the organization as a leader in dealing with outside constituencies. An exemplary article coded in this category described the university as an "international leader in the area of Polymer Technology." This article also discussed how the university was "playing a major role in the revitalization of a declining local economy."

The third cultural dimension category, the *organization's orientation toward time*, included three coding options: *past*, *present*, and *future*. Time *past* statements stressed the value of tradition or encouraged a return to symbols or rituals that had been prominent in the history of the organization. One article coded in this category described the closing of a street running through the center of the urban university as an effort to create "a more traditional campus." Another article praised the defeat of a proposal to change activities of the traditional May Day celebration on the campus. The time *present* coding category was assigned to articles that stressed the need for the organization to deal with the challenges of daily living, rather than relying on past methods or an uncertain future. An example of an article coded in this category described the urgent efforts of university administrators pressuring the city council to enforce more stringent housing codes. This action followed a fire in an off-campus student housing facility that resulted in the death of a graduate student.

The time *future* category included statements that dealt with the mobilization of resources for future endeavors or with more abstract visionary concepts. Articles that detailed strategic planning efforts and long-range goal planning were coded in this category. One of the presidents spoke about "forward thinking" and becoming a "prototype of the University of the future." In one article, the president was quoted as inviting the university community to join him in "moving the University into the 21st century."

The fourth cultural dimension category, the *organization's orientation toward activity* contained three coding options: *passive, moderate,* and *active*. Statements coded in the *passive* category exhibited a cautious approach to innovation and low risk-taking. Exemplary of this passive stance were articles that spoke about perceived inaction regarding long-standing campus problems. For instance, an open letter to the president from the student body described the administration's seeming indifference to student needs, including finding adequate on-campus parking and rebuilding a much-needed student union. Activity statements coded as *moderate* exhibited a modicum of risk-taking, weighed against an assessment of possible losses. One administrator spoke of "weighed innovation" as the optimum university stance regarding action. Another example of this category would be the decision to table a proposition until more research could be conducted regarding the plan. Conversely, an *active* code was assigned to articles that described high risk-taking and movement toward innovation. For instance, one article reported a "dramatic increase" in grant monies generating a "research upturn," while another article revealed extensive plans for a "campus building boom" during that year.

The final cultural dimension included in the coding scheme was the *organization's orientation toward relationships*, specifically, the perception of power distribution across personnel ranks. The three coding categories composing this dimension were: *lineality*, *consultative*, and *collaterality*. A *lineality* code was assigned to descriptions of relationships in terms of strict hierarchical divisions. One article in this category announced the creation of the new position of university provost, which would result in restructuring the arts and sciences programs "under the aegis of a single academic officer." This article stressed how the unification of academic programs "under" the provost would strengthen the institution. A *consultative* relational code represented situations where organizational leaders attempted to elicit input from concerned parties prior to final decision making. An example of this category was a report of the president's meeting with Student Senate officers regarding plans for a newly remodeled student union. The article described the president as "open" to student input, but it also stressed that ultimate decisions regarding policies would rest in the hands of the administrative team.

The final coding option in the relational category, *collaterality*, was assigned to articles expressing the value of team work and group decision making. The previous consultative code described relationships that allowed for input, but the "consulted" groups did not actually make the final decision. Conversely, collateral relationships allow for both input and team-negotiated decision making. An example of a collaterality coding decision was an article that described the efforts of a university search committee in which every member had an equal vote on candidates. A quote from one of the president's speeches seemed to invite a collateral participation in the shaping of university policy: "One individual does not run a university, rather, it is a collective effort—an equal partnership."

The specific examples related in this section attempt to clarify the coding scheme used in the analysis of university publications for the purpose of assessing historical cultural penetration in stable and unstable contexts. Next, a brief summary of the investigation's methodological phases, followed by a general discussion of the primary findings, is provided in the following section.

OVERVIEW OF INVESTIGATION PHASES AND FINDINGS

The described methodology attempted to assess organizational cultural penetration and to distinguish between two distinct types of cultures, *stable* and *unstable*. The first methodological phase in this study used open-ended interviews to isolate cultural schemata, while the second phase, the self-report survey, assessed coorientation across ranks regarding salient constructs. Both the interview and the survey facilitated the charting of the *psychological penetration* of cultural constructs. *Sociological* cultural penetration was assessed by stratifying the organizations into three employee levels (administration, faculty, and staff) and three career stages (socialization, performance, and outcome) and then using statistical calculations to pinpoint patterns of unity and differentiation. Finally, *historical* penetration was assessed by analyzing key cultural dimensions appearing in the print communications of the organizations over time. Although much of the analysis involved statistical comparisons, the discussion of results will be presented in general terms, due to space limitations. Further, in an effort to provide a more indepth discussion of the investigation's findings in relation to cultural range and evolution, the reporting of statistical calculations will be kept to a minimum (statistical tables are available from author upon request).

Determining Dimensions of University Culture

A principal components factor analysis with varimax rotation was used to analyze the forty-item *Organizational Dimensions Survey*. After rotation, eleven factors explained 59.5 percent of the total variance. By using a 50/35 decision criterion, eliminating single-item factors, and using a scree test to plot the point at which eigenvalues leveled, a five-factor solution accounting for 42.0 percent of the total variance resulted. The nine variables that structure the first factor reflected themes of vibrancy, optimism, clarity of future direction, and a positive organizational image. Factor one can be described as an expression of collective pride in the present achievements and future goals of the university. Because of its thematic content, the first factor was named *vision*.

The three variables loading on factor two, *productivity*, dealt with aspects of an employee's job performance and the degree of willingness to exert effort on behalf of the organization. The specific survey items assessed agreement on the existence of problems with apathetic employees, faculty productivity, and level of staff industry. A third cultural dimension, *tradition*, represented items that expressed agreement on the importance of tradition, the groping for a tradition, or the lack of a tradition at the university. A fourth factor, describing the influence of external constituencies on university function, was named *destiny*, because it related to the amount of perceived power held by outside groups in shaping university policy. Survey items in this category assessed agreement on the extent of state domination and the ability of the university to shape its own future without undue constraints from outside forces. Finally, factor five was a *mission* dimension with variables that included aspects of the traditional university mission: research, teaching, and service.

Cronbach's (1951) coefficient alpha was computed for each of the five subscales derived from the factor analysis and for the resulting twenty-item *Organizational Dimensions Survey*. Alphas ranged from .45 to .88. Because of the exploratory nature of this investigation, two dimensions having relatively low reliabilities (destiny and mission) were retained for analysis, so findings relevant to these dimensions should be viewed with caution. However, a relatively high coefficient alpha of .83 computed for the *instrument* may indicate internal consistency and suggest potential as a measurement in future studies. Table 6.1 summarizes the core unitary dimensions, isolated in this investigation, which may be generalizable across contexts other than universities. The dimensions that define an organization's unitary culture are a composite of factors characterizing its *vision, mission, tradition, destiny,* and *productivity*. Native perceptions of evaluative cultural dimensions result in distinct patterns of contextual stability and instability.

As we have noted, the primary research question proposed in this investigation asked which of the dependent variables would best discriminate between stable and unstable cultures. A stepwise multiple discriminant analysis was conducted using stable and unstable cultures as criterion variables and the five cultural dimensions and identification as predictor variables. Appendix F, "Summary of Stepwise Multiple Discriminant Analysis," summarizes the results of the procedure. A total of 77.7 percent of the cases were correctly classified, with 78.4 percent classified in the unstable culture and 77.0 percent correctly classified in the stable culture. A significant canonical discriminant function was derived from the analysis, Rc = .61, eigenvalue = .60, Wilk's lambda = .63, X^2 (5, N = 421) = 192.52, p < .001. Based on an analysis of structure coefficients, *mission* and *vision* appeared to be the best discriminators between the two cultures.

TABLE 6.1
Core Unitary Dimensions of an Organizational Culture

Dimension	*Characterized by Perceptions of...*
Vision	innovation action growth and change shaping external environment organizational direction future orientation peer institutions' perception
Mission	primary reason for operating
Tradition	achieving balance between past and present
Destiny	maintaining autonomy amidst control of outside forces
Productivity	work level of personnel

In this chapter, we have discussed the phases of a research investigation of organizational culture in university contexts. Chapter 7 will present implications of the results derived from statistical analysis of the hypotheses, research question, and content analysis data. The commentary will detail how the study assessed cultural range by tracing psychological, sociological, and historical penetration of salient cultural dimensions. In addition, the chapter will provide two ethnographic portraits of stable and unstable cultures, drawn from composites that reflect results derived from the use of quantitative and qualitative methods in the triphase investigation.

Chapter 7

CULTURAL RANGE AND STABILITY

*Culture's real value as a "new" variable in the field, may lie
in its face validity and the degree to which it seems to capture previously, seemingly ineffable organizational attributes that researchers and practitioners alike agree are there.*
—*A. Reichers and B. Schneider*

The empirical investigation described in these two chapters explores the development of a theoretically grounded conceptualization of organizational culture and proposes a method
for measurement of cultural range and stability. Organizational
culture was conceptualized in this investigation as a multidimensional cognitive phenomenon composed of collectively
shared value orientations regarding human nature, the environment, time, activity, and relationships in organizational
contexts (Child 1981; Kluckhohn & Stodtbeck 1961). It was proposed in this study that in order to best measure organizational
culture the sociological, psychological, and historical penetration of cultural constructs must be assessed (Louis 1985a,
1985b). The triangulated methodology used in this investigation enables researchers to assess agreement on core cultural
schemata (psychological penetration), across organizational
levels (sociological penetration), and over time (historical penetration). Taken together, these measures provide a composite
picture of the stability or instability of a particular cultural

milieu. The ensuing discussion focuses on the investigation's assessment of cultural range, while the latter portion of the chapter will present summaries of major findings by providing ethnographic portraits of stable and unstable cultural contexts.

TRACING CULTURAL RANGE

Psychological Cultural Penetration

An assessment of psychological cultural penetration, the collective agreement on core cultural dimensions, was accomplished in this investigation by the creation and testing of a self-report measure. The *Organizational Dimensions Survey* was designed to assess agreement on core cultural dimensions. As we have seen in the last chapter, results of the factor analysis of the ODS produced a twenty-item scale composed of five dimensions: *vision, mission, tradition, destiny,* and *productivity.* All of the cultural dimensions in the scale are universal in scope and represent relevant organizational issues in a variety of contexts.

As previously noted and summarized in table 6.1, the cultural dimensions in this study were composites of the five cultural dimensions drawn from the literature. *Vision* was composed of items from the human nature, environment, time, activity, and culture dimensions; these items represented feelings of pride and confidence in the future of the organization. Perceptions of innovation, movement in a positive direction, and active involvement in shaping the local community were orientations indicative of the vision dimension. The *mission* dimension described the varying perceptions across the organization, regarding the primary reason for the institution to operate.

Tradition represented items depicting the primacy of past norms in the organization; was there a perception across ranks that an optimum balance between past and present was maintained? *Destiny* consisted of three items from the theoretical environment dimension that described perceptions of the organization's amount of control over outside forces. The destiny dimension dealt with the impact of environmental forces on the university and the problem of maintaining autonomy while dealing with imposed sanctions of outside forces. For example, in this study, state governments were examples of outside constraining forces that often imposed inhibiting regulations on the universities. Finally, the *productivity* dimension encompassed perceptions of personnel work levels throughout the organization. The dimensional orientations in this study share some similarities with cultural dimensions isolated by other researchers in their investigations of university contexts. For instance, Treadwell's (1987) image dimensions of "mission," "reputation," and "conservatism," cited in his study of a small liberal arts college community, resemble the mission, destiny, and time dimensions found in this investigation. Harris and Cronen's (1979) exploration of coorientation on organizational image in an academic department revealed four similar constructs: "bright faculty versus deadwood," "capable versus inept administrative leadership," "power versus powerlessness," and "local service versus research mission." These constructs share similarities with the productivity, destiny, and mission dimensions in this study.

In summary, the *Organizational Dimensions Survey* developed and tested in this field investigation, provides a tool for assessing the psychological penetration of culture by measuring the collective contextual agreement on core cultural dimensions. This tool also provides a way to distinguish a stable from an unstable culture. Configurations of the evaluative dimensions found in stable and unstable contexts illustrate how natives of each distinct organizational culture view reality and approach problems. The distinctive patterns of values etched upon both university contexts will be discussed in greater depth, as two portraits of cultural stability are revealed in the latter portion of this chapter. The next section will describe how data gathered from use of the ODS was analyzed to chart another aspect of cultural range—sociological penetration.

Sociological Cultural Penetration

Sociological penetration of an organizational culture is a measure of the extent of collective agreement on core cultural dimensions across organizational levels. As we noted in the theoretical discussion in part 1, organizational cultures may exhibit some stable unitary sharing of salient dimensions across ranks; however, patterns of differentiation regarding agreement on the official corporate cultural dictates characterize most contexts. This investigation provided assessments of the sociological penetration of culture across organizational levels (administration, faculty, staff) and at career stages (socialization, performance, outcome). In general, results showed differences in levels of agreement across both organizations, regarding core cultural dimensions.

For example, administration and staff both exhibited significantly higher means on the vision scale than did faculty. These results are consistent when viewed in the light of recent press coverage reporting very low faculty morale at University A (unstable culture). Although the faculty mean at University B (stable culture) was significantly lower for vision than administration or staff means, it still outranked that of the faculty at the unstable institution, thereby exhibiting more cohesion on vision. Other significant differences for level were found on dimensions of tradition and mission. The staff at both universities perceived themselves to be more traditional than did the administration or the faculty. Perhaps in their enactment of daily duties they may have experienced more continuity and less variety in tasks, thereby creating a feeling of security in their particular university function. Also, some of the staff may have been involved officially in the planning or implementation of "traditional" campus activities such as registration, grade processing, or commencement. Staff members were also not likely to have participated in strategic planning efforts or to have been on the cutting edge of university or departmental innovations.

Another area of difference between the staff and other organizational levels was on the mission dimension. The administration of both the stable and unstable cultures differed significantly from staff on the importance of the university mission. The two items that constituted this dimension referred to the teaching and research mission of the university, both of which had little relevance for staff members. Differentiation in the organizational cultures according to rank was also evident in the finding that at each university the administration had significantly higher levels of organizational identification than did faculty and staff. Because the administrators in both organizations possessed some power in determining both the image and the fate of the university, it is not surprising that this group would tend to identify more highly with the organization that they were actively managing.

In summarizing the findings regarding organizational level differences, it is useful to consider the results in terms of theoretical descriptions of stable and unstable cultures. For instance, Schein (1985) suggested that the amount of consensus regarding organizational schemata indicate whether a coherent cultural paradigm does in fact exist in an organizational context. Similarly, Van Maanen and Barley (1985) posited that if there is much overlap and tight clustering among subcultural belief systems, there is evidence for the existence of an organizational culture. In this investigation, three broad subcultures of administration, faculty, and staff were delineated. In measuring the sociological penetration of culture by charting significant differences in agreement regarding core cultural dimensions at differing organizational levels, a researcher should be able to determine if there is some evidence of a unitary culture. Contrary to expectations of agreement on cultural dimensions at all levels for the stable culture, the faculty mean at the stable culture was significantly lower on vision than were the administration or staff means. Although this finding shows that level differences do exist in the stable culture, it also reflects the faculty/administration differences of opinion often existing in university cultures in general.

In addition to level in the organization, another way in which the sociological penetration of culture may be assessed is through an examination of structural differences regarding perception of cultural dimensions according to career stages. In this particular investigation, however, no significant differences in perception of cultural dimensions for employees at the socialization (one year), performance (two to four years), and outcome (five years and longer) stages of employment were found. In the university contexts selected, it seemed that level in the organization, rather than number of years employed, influenced the perception of cultural dimensions. In business contexts outside of academia, more highly structured socialization programs would likely play a key role in shaping an employee's perception of and identification with corporate cultural dimensions throughout career stages.

The two previous sections have presented an overview of implications present in the results of psychological and sociological assessments of culture in organizations. The final portion of this summary of research implications regarding cultural range will examine findings related to the historical penetration of culture.

Historical Cultural Penetration

Penetration of cultural constructs across time is another indication of the strength and stability of an organizational culture. In this study, a content analysis methodology was used to trace the stability of theoretical cultural constructs (human nature, environment, time, activity, relationships) across two time periods in organizational history. The time periods selected for this study were time period one, three years prior to the new president's appointment in the unstable culture, and time period two, the first three years of the new president's administration in the unstable culture. The six-year time period encompassed the entire term of the president in the stable culture with time period one being the initial three years after his inauguration and time period two covering the most recent years of service. It was predicted that there would be less fluctuation in value orientations regarding cultural dimensions, as exhibited in the print publications of the stable culture, because a consistent vision and mission had been promulgated. Conversely, more dramatic fluxes in value orientations regarding cultural dimensions were expected in the print matter of the unstable culture, since the new president was involved in the process of articulating a novel cultural vision at the time of the investigation.

Contrary to the predictions, chi-square calculations showed significant differences in cultural orientations for all dimensions in the stable culture and for three of the five dimensions in the unstable culture. General results pertaining to the stable culture indicated that, for the *human nature dimension*, there was a significant trend toward more coverage showcasing the *good* aspects of individuals in the university community. The *environmental dimension* revealed a significant shift from a *subjugation* orientation to a *control* orientation. Also, the *time dimension* showed a significant increase in coverage emphasizing a *future* orientation rather than a *past* orientation, with a move toward an *active* as opposed to a *passive* orientation. Finally, a significant decrease in *lineality*, a highly structured hierarchy and an increase in *collaterality*, shared decision making, was noted for the cultural dimension of *relational orientation*. Rather than a stable culture maintaining the status quo, it seems, at least in analyzing print coverage, that there was a definite trend toward innovation and change. Perhaps the clarity regarding vision and mission that characterizes stable cultures may be strengthened by transformational leaders who are willing to take risks in increasing innovation and decentralizing power across the organization.

In the stable culture, the growing shift toward a *human nature good* orientation in the print coverage tended to reinforce corporate cultural values by giving praise to individuals acting out officially sanctioned norms. As mentioned, significantly more coverage exhibiting a *control* over the environment orientation was found during time period two in the stable context. This tendency can be explained by the fact that the stable culture was accorded more autonomy by the state during the latter portion of the president's tenure. During his first three years in office, the university was plagued by severe budget cuts and strict regulation regarding policy by state government officials. It is hardly surprising, then, that the first three years of the president's term were characterized by significantly high levels of coverage having a *subjugation* orientation. In addition, the increased coverage reflecting *collaterality*, paralleled administrative efforts to decentralize bureaucratic functions and to launch more team efforts characterized by shared decision making.

By way of contrast, the print coverage in the unstable cultural context revealed significant shifts in time, activity, and relational orientations. Very dramatic shifts from a *past* to a *future* orientation and from a *passive* to an *active* orientation were evident for *time* and *activity dimensions*. These findings were consistent with the new president's accelerated, persistent efforts to expand the scope of the university's mission. The significant shifts toward *future* and *active* orientations in the print coverage of the unstable culture also reflected descriptions of growth and succession stage cultures in the literature (Cameron & Whetten, 1981; Schein 1985). In addition, the unstable culture had significant differences in its press coverage for the relational dimension; a shift from a *collaterality* orientation in time period one to a *lineality* orientation in time period two was noted.

Unlike the president in the stable culture, who sought to distribute power across the ranks through decentralization, the president in the unstable, succession culture launched efforts to centralize university departments by restructuring the ranks. The print coverage for time period two in the unstable culture contained numerous stories detailing the president's reorganization of administrative ranks, the creation of new administrative posts, and descriptions of new hierarchical structures. As we have noted, the shift from *collaterality* to *lineality* in the unstable culture ran counter to the finding for the print coverage of the stable culture, which revealed a significant shift toward initiatives to promote decentralization and increase horizontal communiration. The trend in the stable culture to mobilize team-oriented approaches reflects Mintzberg's (1983) suggestion that mature cultures tend to maintain more even power distribution through organizational ranks.

These findings analyzing print records of each university context over time parallel theoretical models of the evolutionary stages of organizational cultures evident in contemporary literature. Also, the fluctuating value orientations in both stable and unstable contexts portray culture as a dynamic, ever-changing phenomenon that plays a key role in organizational growth processes. This section has discussed the results of the investigation in terms of the psychological, sociological, and historical range of cultural dimensions in dual stable and unstable contexts. The next section will collate the major findings by creating portraits of cultural stability in light of distinctive characteristics.

PORTRAITS OF CULTURAL STABILITY

The cultural portraits presented in this section consist of general characteristics regarding stable and unstable cultures drawn from both the quantitative and qualitative data gathered during the three phases of this investigation: interview, survey, and content analysis. Since the interview phase was conducted only on the upper administrative level, most of the quotes included in this discussion represent an administration viewpoint. However, faculty and staff survey participants were invited to submit open-ended written comments pertaining to items on the *Organizational Dimensions Survey*. These comments are included in the portraits wherever appropriate to illustrate cultural orientations held by personnel in both universities. The items listed in table 7.1 summarize the characteristics of both stable and unstable cultural milieu, as noted in the context of this field investigation. Also, the summary listings provide an overview of the main ideas discussed in this section.

The Stable Organizational Culture

The hallmark of a stable cultural context is clarity regarding an organizational vision and mission. In this investigation, the cultural dimension of vision was characterized by widespread agreement across ranks that the organization was headed in a positive direction, while the mission dimension revealed a consistency about the present goals pursued in the stable context. Under the transformational leadership of the president and administrative team, the stable culture exhibited continued growth toward innovation by maintaining collective *future* value orientations. Also, natives of the stable culture perceived themselves as triumphing over subjugation to attain greater collective control over the destiny of the university. This steadily intensifying "bright future" stance was aptly described in interviews and in print matter. One administrator spoke of a "shared perception of vibrant growth and change." Another administrator commented on a sense of pride in being employed by the university: "People want to work for a winner." A comment that seemed to summarize the cohesion regarding vision was: "The fact that we're moving ahead is something everyone can relate to—that aspect is the shared culture."

TABLE 7.1
Cultural Characteristics of Stable and Unstable Contexts

Stable Contexts Tend to Exhibit...
Clarity on core organizational vision and mission
Positive tone regarding present developments
Tendency to view tradition with moderation
Unification of ranks against a perceived collective challenge
Leader who actively promotes positive aspects of organization and its people
Leader who encourages collective action
Leader who articulates a universal theme in print and oral communications

Unstable Contexts Tend to Exhibit...
Disagreement and/or confusion regarding core vision and mission
Marked increase in activity levels
Major restructuring across ranks
High uncertainty levels within subcultures
Clinging to "traditions" that thwart innovation
Perceived disparity among subcultures
Low morale at key organizational levels

As we have mentioned, stable cultures also attain marked clarity regarding the organization's primary mission. Traditionally, in academic contexts, urban university missions were frequently built around a high level of community involvement. The culture of the stable university context did indeed reflect such a vigilance for the well being of the adjacent community. For instance, one administrator described the "obligation" of the public university to repair the "failing economy" in the local community. He added that the "engineering, medical school, management, architecture, and natural sciences are renovating the local financial base most noticeably." Another comment noted that in the last decade the university had succeeded in moving from the "edge of involvement with the community" to the "center of community involvement." A recent article about University B in a national news magazine confirmed administrative comments regarding the

University's seeming "heroic" role in community revitalization. The article described the acquisition of a prestigious grant establishing a coveted national research center on the urban campus. Also, the print article accorded the grant a "symbolic importance" in a university-wide effort to "pull the local economy out of the Rust Belt doldrums."

Another important component of mission in the stable culture is the collective agreement on the priority of research in the university. One of the administrators interviewed, described the research mission in lofty terms: "Graduates of good research institutions are essential to the furtherance of civilization." He added that although "lofty," it was not an "unreal goal" for the institution. Another administrator spoke of the "obsession" to secure external funds for faculty research. This primacy of research was described by other administrators as the "dominant and distinguishing" mission that "gives a special cast and character to the teaching of the university." In one of his annual addresses to the academic community, the president conveyed the idea that he was "very impressed" by the fact that "all of our con-stituents appear to have a remarkably clear conception of the mission of this university."

A second distinctive characteristic of stable cultures seems to be a positive tone regarding the present functioning of the organization. Often, this attitude could be described as a perception that the present is better than the past. This type of positive stance was evident in interviews with administrators and random comments from faculty and staff. One administrator noted that in the past some university employees "kept reinforcing a system of negatives," whereas present-ly "the emphasis is on positives, on things that people can identify with." Another comment of this type was: "Things that people used to think were problems have been put into perspective." One of the administrators observed that seemingly negative occurrences were viewed from a more positive perspective now: "We're not trying to be all things to all people; we have a greater understanding of our situa-tion." A comment that encompasses the tenor of this optimistic yet moderate stance stated: "There is a stronger sense of—this is what we are at this point in time."

A third characteristic evident in the stable culture in this investi-gation is the tendency to be "moderately" traditional. Although tradi-tion was viewed as a positive element in the organization, the admin-istrators who were interviewed stressed that tradition in University B was "not stifling." One of the administrators claimed that tradition was "approached from a tasteful balance, not oppressive." Another administrator felt that the university was not "preoccupied with tradition" but was, rather, "modestly innovative." It is also interesting to note that survey results showed that the unstable culture had significantly higher agreement regarding the importance of tradition than did the stable culture. Much of the instability taking place at University A was fueled by an affinity for the past, evident across the ranks of the organization. Change initiatives launched by the president in the unstable context were consistently thwarted, particularly within faculty ranks, thus making transformational leadership to alter the culture close to impossible. On the other hand, the stable culture's president was attempting to promote core unitary values by reinstating some of the university's "lost traditions" that had fallen by the wayside as the campus increased in size and scope.

The cohesion created by uniting the ranks against a common "enemy" is a fourth characteristic of a stable cultural context. As previously noted, Cheney (1983b) described an identification by "antithesis" in which employees perceived themselves as collectively battling a prospective threat to their organization. Content analysis of print matter revealed a gradual evolution in the stable culture from a perception of state subjugation toward a greater degree of collective control over threatening outside forces. One administrator suggested that university employees had made a "tradition of uncertainty" in their ongoing battle with the state bureaucracy. In the stable university context, the yearly "battle of the budget" had actually functioned to unite employees at all ranks for nearly three decades. As one veteran administrator noted wryly: "We certainly have spent a lot of years fighting among ourselves as to whether we should love the state, hate the state or respect the state, and I think that's going to go on for quite a while longer."

A fifth characteristic of a stable culture noted in the investigation is the presence of a leader who actively acknowledges and promotes the good aspects of the organization. Administrative comments about the president included descriptions of his expertise as both a "cheerleader" and a "salesman" for the university. In the words of one administrator, the president possessed the "ability to recognize the wonderful things done by faculty, students, and staff, and package it and sell it." A national news magazine noted that the "aggressive leadership" of the president had brought "new vigor" to a community that had "ceased to believe in its ability to garner favorable national attention." Transformational leaders in complex contemporary organizations frequently call attention to individual accomplishments in order to create heroes who serve to reinforce corporate-sanctioned values.

In addition to focusing favorable attention on the accomplishments of the organization and its people, a sixth characteristic of a stable culture seems to be that the leader takes steps to promote collective action. In the perception of his fellow administrators, University B's president has sought to create a more cohesive culture by establishing "focal points" that would "eliminate separations." As examples of these unification efforts, the administrators cited the appointment of a single academic officer (provost), the establishment of a single phone system, the revival of a single commencement, and the issuance of strict guidelines for university publications, stating how the university should be described in print materials. These attempts by University B's president to actively manage the organization's "corporate" culture aptly exemplify concepts of "transactional management" (Burns 1978) and "cultural intervention" (Lundberg 1985), where administrators provide viable and consistent symbols at the normative and artifactual levels to unify disparate elements in the organization.

A seventh characteristic of a stable culture is frequent public reference to a universal conceptual theme that can be collectively embraced by diverse constituencies across the organization. The stable culture in this investigation adopted the well-known excellence concept that is reflective of numerous contemporary corporate cultures. Reference to excellence appeared consistently in internally and externally disseminated print vehicles and in direct quotes from the public addresses of the president. For instance, University B's president entitled his annual State of the University address to the academic community, "Choosing Excellence." In another address, he spoke about the "excellence of our faculty" and the striving for "academic excellence." Analysis of University B's administrative interviews revealed frequent reference to the excellence theme. For example, one administrator seemed to describe excellence as a way of unifying diverse factions: "You must embrace a philosophy of excellence here, no matter what your standpoint." Another administrator stressed that excellence was an "obligation" for members of this academic community: "Excellence is underscored—we have the responsibility to promote excellence." As we have noted in the corporate culture literature, themes having universal appeal for all levels of the organization, such as excellence or quality, assist transformational leaders in creating strong unitary cultures.

These general characteristics paint a picture of a stable culture as an organization having clarity regarding its vision and mission. In addition, stable cultures tend to have a positive perception of present developments, and they avoid an inordinate resistance to change. Rather than expending energy on widespread internal conflict, stable cultures derive some cohesion throughout organizational ranks by unification against a common external challenge. Finally, the transformational leadership in the stable culture publicly recognizes individual accomplishments, provides viable symbols of unification, and promotes a universally relevant concept, such as excellence, as a unifying cultural theme.

In contemporary cultural descriptions, several researchers have discussed characteristics that resemble the stable culture in this investigation. For instance, Akin and Hopelain (1988) delineated the essential qualities of a "culture of productivity" as legible, coherent, and open-ended. In this type of situation, clearly articulated cultural norms and values are integrated within a context that adapts to change. Denison (1990) also stressed the need for value consistency and a clear definition of the organization's mission. In determining criteria for organizational performance and effectiveness, Denison endorsed a balance between flexibility and stability. Consistent with Ouchi's (1980) "clan" hypothesis, effective organizations blend shared values and meaningful traditions to foster high levels of employee involvement. As Limerick (1990) has noted, leaders in complex, loosely coupled organizations, such as universities, need to rely more strongly on shared goals, values, and meanings to secure collaborative action.

The Unstable Organizational Culture

The unstable culture in this study typified an institution in a developmental stage of succession (Schein 1985). In the cultural growth stage of succession, a new leader replaces a well-established administrator. In unstable contexts, intensified levels of energy and activity paradoxically create dual problems and potentialities. The seven characteristics of unstable cultures proposed in this section describe some of the challenges generated by succession situations (see table 7.1). A number of the characteristics of the unstable culture in this investigation are closely interrelated, so rather than approaching this discussion chronologically, we will touch upon the interaction of these elements.

A predominant theme that appears consistently in a portrait of the unstable culture is the inevitable presence of change, coupled with increased activity levels. In the words of one administrator, "We're coming out of a plateau of inertia; we're not at all satisfied with the way we are now." A veteran administrator attempted to lend a perspective on the recent surge of activity on campus: "The tempo around here has changed—ten years ago we were cautious and laid back, but now we're close to hyper-active." The surges of activity required to mount the structural and functional changes that were initiated by the newly appointed president resulted in higher levels of uncertainty that proved threatening to certain segments of the organization. The transformational leadership strategies designed to introduce changes in organizational vision and mission that appeared to be highly successful in the stable culture were met with resistance and suspicion in the unstable context.

One of the most notable changes taking place in University A with the advent of the new administration was an alteration in the mission of the organization. The president was attempting to expand the "traditional" university mission from primarily a local focus to one of national scope. Although the alteration was not meant to deemphasize local affiliations, the administration's perceived change of the traditional community service initiative aroused fear in some employees. One of the upper-level administrators referred to a widespread perceived internal "threat" on the part of certain faculty and staff due to the recent tremendous changes. Survey comments of faculty members questioned the wisdom of the president's efforts to secure a national reputation for the university through an expanded football program. In the interview, one of the veteran administrators who had served the university for two decades observed that the recent "quest" for a "national image" could become potentially "dangerous" by taking the university "away from its roots." A member of the new adminstrative team attributed resistance to mission alterations by describing the campus as being, "in another era—immobile and resistant to change." Similarly, another newly hired team member observed that the university "needs to be pushed to do what it should do."

One of the specific groups in the university cited by administrators as being "change resistant" was faculty. An administrator noted ironically that although faculty could be "very innovative" in their departments, they tended to "resist change in the university." Other administrators commented with chagrin on the attempt of some faculty to "actively sabotage goals" but concluded that this was to be expected as a normal occurrence in a change situation. The marked levels of confusion or outright disagreement with an expanding university vision and mission seemed to be fueled by massive restructuring across ranks and an increased level of activity that some constituencies found threatening.

Another prominent characteristic of the unstable culture that emerges from interview and survey comments is a sense of dissatisfaction and low morale at key levels in the organizational structure. As noted in the previous discussion on resistance to change, faculty emerged as a group showing strong negative feelings about new administrative policies. One of the controversial policies initiated by the new administration was more stringent evaluation procedures. In the words of one administrator: "Frequent evaluation of individuals, departments, and schools is necessary to maintain high-quality performance." While administrators saw evaluation procedures as an effort to upgrade institutional quality, some faculty seemed to perceive evaluative measures as an attack. One angry faculty member added several handwritten statements to the bottom of the *Organizational Dimensions Survey* that spoke of a feeling of collective frustration among faculty: "Faculty members need a union to secure a collective bargaining unit soon." Another of the written statements strongly asserted that the current president and provost "are disasters." In addition, the faculty had submitted a proposal to the board of trustees requesting stringent evaluation of the president and provost.

Another faculty member in University A offered advice to the administration in this written comment on the survey: "Support the faculty, don't put them down, override, and humiliate them as is done." A similar feeling was expressed in yet another faculty comment: "Morale is in the pits here!" In another comment on the survey, a faculty member admonished the administration for not "rewarding" and "recognizing" faculty efforts. By contrast, during his six-year term, the president at the stable institution steadily increased public mention of positive individual contributions in print and oral communications to the university community. To stem the tide of increasing resistance to cultural innovation, the president in the unstable context would be wise to pay heed to the growing intensity of critical commentary and to weigh further introduction of innovation against prevailing subcultural values and norms.

Although it appeared more intense in the unstable context, the perceived gap between faculty and administrative subcultures may be characteristic of university environments in general. For example, in a written comment on the survey, one faculty member (University B) described the essential difference in this way: "My perception is that administrators do not run this University, committees of faculty do. I don't particularly like the administrators I know. Their interests are different from mine. They chose administration, while I chose quite consciously not to be an administrator." Similarly, one of the administrators (University B) observed that "management is an anathema to many faculty members—they don't like to think of themselves as being managed." An administrator from University A perceived that faculty lack "the same kind of institutional loyalty or identity" as most administrators possess and added that the faculty are "generally unwilling to enhance the image of the university."

While some conflict between faculty and administrative subcultures tends to create an "energizing" differentiation in the university cultural milieu, the stable university context reveals diverse organizational levels collectively sharing perceptions of the university's core vision and mission. However, from the comments recorded in analysis of the unstable culture, it is evident that the high levels of perceived disparity between administration and faculty resulted in increasing amounts of conflict and the subverting of administrative efforts to implement strategic innovations. This observation is consistent with Schein's (1985) concept of "succession" growth stage cultures as "battlegrounds" between liberals and conservatives. A comment by one of the administrators in the unstable culture described this conflict: "This University has a conservative nature; we're currently bringing in people with more liberal ideas."

Another administrator described the conflict as being between "people who have been here who feel that they own the institution" and the newly appointed "outsiders" who are not perceived as "a part of the family." One staff member referred to a formerly used metaphor of the university as "family" in a written comment on the survey: "We no longer have a feeling of family where everyone is acquainted; I guess it's hard to keep this feeling in a large university, and some people who have been here a long time feel a sense of loss." In this particular university, problems that naturally occur in succession stage cultures were intensified, in part, because the new president succeeded a highly popular figure who had come up through the ranks to attain leadership status.

Closely allied to several of the characteristics described so far is a clinging to tradition that seemed to permeate the unstable culture in this context. This observation is consistent with results showing significantly higher means denoting a *past* orientation for the unstable culture on the tradition dimension. One of the new administrative team observed that decision making was being severely hindered by precedent. In his estimation, this reliance on precedent "stood in the way" of needed innovation. Another member of the new administrative team stressed that now more decisions were being made according to strategic goals rather than precedent. However, this particular administrator recalled incidents in which the "new team" had "held back" on a decision, fearing that "it would cause too much uproar." Although fairly high levels of organizational identification were present in the unstable context, analysis of findings led to the conclusion that many of the natives were aligning themselves with the "culture of the past," rather than with the newly articulated vision and its resulting normative values.

In summary, seven interrelated elements blend together to create the portrait of an unstable cultural context described in this section. The unstable university culture in this investigation exhibited sharply increased levels of activity, fueled by major restructuring in normative policy, that resulted, ultimately, in a fear of change that crossed all organizational levels. These forces, in turn, led to disagreement and confusion regarding corporate vision and mission, thwarting leadership attempts at transformation of collective cultural values. As in many succession cultures, there is perceived disparity among groups, resulting in low morale at key organizational levels. Finally, a marked clinging to tradition fostered organizational identification with a comfortable, nostalgic past, rather than alignment with an unfamiliar, risk-oriented, corporate culture.

In two investigations of academic contexts, Cameron (1986a, 1986b) analyzed factors that account for improvement of organizational effectiveness. While Cameron suggested that a leader's attention to symbol management was a key factor in the survival of institutions challenged by decline, it becomes equally important to balance new leadership with the stability of trusted administrators already established in the context in order for innovations to succeed. The blending of new ideas with the preservation of history seems to exemplify the moderately traditional stance of the stable culture in this investigation. Organizations that reinforced and perpetuated a core cultural saga, while concurrently introducing innovations and creative activity, were more effective in Cameron's estimation.

Additionally, organizational leaders face the precarious challenge of confronting internal morale issues while reacting to external demands. The president in the unstable culture in this study was beset with growing internal morale problems while attempting to promote a more viable image of the university with outside constituencies. Leaders in unstable contexts are often plagued with double-bind situations involving the amount of energy they can afford to expend on internal relational difficulties versus the intensified energy levels required to articulate their new cultural visions. It would seem that, in the unstable context, the president walked a tightrope between a transformational leadership style that served to articulate a vision and a transactional managment initiative that launched massive value changes at normative and artifactual levels. If fragmentation across the ranks in the unstable culture is not alleviated, however, the president will have little chance of success in making a corporate-level vision collective.

Cyclical Challenges of Cultural Stability

As we have noted in discussing the evolutionary stages of culture, the concept of 'cultural stablity' as described in this investigation has some support in the literature. Schein's (1985) description of organizations in the "maturity" stage characterized by internal stability is similar to the stable culture in this study. Likewise, Cameron and Whetten (1981) referred to a "collectivity" state in the life cycle of an organizational culture. Most of the descriptions of collective or stable cultures, however, include the aspect of inflexibility due to firmly institutionalized practices. For instance, Caplow (1983) noted that some stable organizations might be resistant to change. Unlike these theoretical descriptions, the stable culture in this study showed signs of growth and change. As Schein noted, if "mature" cultures preserve core assumptions while maintaining flexibility, then stagnation may be averted. The term *stable* as used in this investigation, then, differs from Caplow's (1983) definition of a stable organization as one that is neither growing nor declining. According to the dimensions isolated in this study, a stable culture is characterized by positive acceptance of organizational innovation coupled with a strong conviction of a "bright future" ahead.

The unstable culture in this investigation resembled closely Schein's (1985) description of the "succession" phase of a growing culture. In the succession phase, a firmly established leader is succeeded by a "newcomer" to the organization. When the new leader attempts to change accepted practices, the fledgling culture often becomes a battleground between liberals and conservatives. In his "managerial succession" typology, Caplow (1983) predicted that an outside successor following a strong predecessor would have a moderately favorable chance of administrative success. Caplow advised the successor to develop a personal style that contrasts sharply with that of the former organizational leader but to retain the policies that contribute to the strength of the organization. In other words, the new leader can avoid being compared to a predecessor by being so different in style as to defy comparison. However, Caplow also advised restructuring the existing hierarchy to create favorable alliances for the new administration.

The behavior of the president in the *unstable* culture appears to be consistent with Caplow's (1983) ideas regarding succession. However, in the process of restructuring, the new president overlooked the necessity of identifying core values of the existing strong culture before introducing massive innovations. For instance, the metaphor of family emerged as a key value both in interviews and in written comments, yet the new president seemed to ignore this concept in his communication with the campus community. Pfeffer (1981) suggested that successful administrative actions induce behavioral compliance and enhance positive sentiments to the extent that their symbolic content is consistent with existing norms and values.

Leaders have a greater chance for success in introducing reforms if they build on existing symbolic content and value systems. Also, successors need to be apprised of the influential people at all levels of the organization who may represent traditional values. For instance, Deal and Kennedy (1982) warned new leaders not to attack unwittingly "priests" and "priestesses" of the existing culture in their efforts to introduce innovation. In eliminating certain personnel at the university, the administration in the unstable context may have appeared to challenge certain strongly held values. According to Schein (1985), the tendency to revert to a past orientation in the face of rapid growth and change provides a sense of security for natives mired in an environment of high uncertainty. However, an organizational culture grounded in the preservation of "past glories" lacks both the relevance and the energy needed to meet present and future needs.

A finding that seems to suggest that the unstable culture will progress toward stabilization under its new leadership is the significant level of agreement regarding a control orientation on the *destiny* dimension. The fact that the unstable culture perceives itself to be in control of its destiny despite current turmoil provides the organization with dynamic growth potential. Cameron and Whetten's (1981) description of the first stage in cultural life cycles, termed "creativity and entrepreneurship," contains elements of this dynamic control orientation. An innovation that may eventually win the president greater support with both internal and external constituencies appears to be his negotiations with the city to complete a structural bridge linking downtown businesses directly to the main campus. While this ambitious plan had been the object of lengthy debate for more than a decade with the previous administration, no action had taken place. Taking innovative action that reinforces one of the more strongly held values of the prior university culture—localized community service—should assist the new president in increasing the degree of collective support.

Notes of Closure—Portending the Future

The previous sections have discussed major findings of an empirical investigation of organizational culture, by focusing on tracing the range and stability of cultural dimensions within two contexts of differing evolutionary stages, stable and unstable. This investigation represents an attempt to develop and test a theoretically derived measure of organizational culture. The methodological model presented in this study allows researchers to surface existing cultural dimensions and to assess cultural range across organizational strata over time. Preliminary results indicate that the *Organizational Dimensions Survey (ODS)* may provide a starting point from which to develop viable tools for researchers assessing the psychological, sociological, and historical penetration of cultural dimensions in organizational contexts.

The five dimensions of culture forming the basis of the ODS (*vision, mission, tradition, destiny,* and *productivity*) portray organizational culture as a multidimensional cognitive construct. The characteristics of stable and unstable cultural milieu derived from this investigation will provide working models that assist researchers and administrators in charting evolutionary stages of their organizational cultures. By identifying distinct configurations of value orientations that characterize cultural contexts, administrators can better achieve an optimum balance of transactional managerial interventions to alter existing norms and artifacts with the visionary transformational strategies to collectively articulate organizational vision. In considering several of the key concepts in this empirical investigation, chapter 8 will provide an agenda for further research. Also, we will focus on emerging trends related to the future of organizational culture research in general.

Chapter 8

MERGING ORGANIZATIONAL REALITY WITH COLLECTIVE VISION: A RESEARCH AGENDA

What then, is an organizational culture? It can be an umbrella concept for clinical-minded researchers. Further, it can be a new control rhetoric, or even a managerial ideology. Alternatively, culture can be an analytical concept to use in organizations...Its positive aspect is that the slogan 'pluralism in research' begins to sound as if it were really possible.
—B. Czarniawska-Joerges

Part 1 of this volume examined the ever-growing body of literature in the area of organizational culture, and set forth some issues of importance in construct evolution. The empirical investigation reported in part 2, illustrates the challenges involved in identifying a set of core value orientations and charting the range and stability of cultural dimensions in organizational contexts. This chapter will provide closure by first presenting several future research directions emanating from implications of the field study. Finally, we will consider a number of issues that are raised in contemporary literature regarding the organizational culture construct that create future research agendas.

FIELD EXPLORATION OF CULTURE—IMPLICATIONS AND EXPANSIONS

As we have seen in part 1, a primary goal for organizational culture researchers is achieving some modicum of consensus regarding a definition of the construct. When culture investigations are grounded in shared theoretical conceptualizations and methodological operationalizations, the capacity to compare and generalize findings across organizational contexts will become a reality. The challenge of future investigations is to embrace a more holistic view of the construct by providing for multidimensional, multilevel analyses.

In order for more holistic analyses to occur, it is essential to identify the cognitive dimensions that emanate from underlying organizational assumptions. These interpretive schemes are rooted in "universal" dimensions based on value orientations that cut across organizational contexts. For instance, the triangulated field investigation detailed in the last two chapters isolated several factors similar to anthropological dimensions that cross cultural contexts. As stated in the discussion of the findings, dimensions such as vision, productivity, destiny, and tradition represent orientations that may exist in many cultural groups.

Contextual dimensions, however, are unique to a particular context and may distinguish one organizational culture from another. In the university case study, for instance, the distinctive mission dimension was perceived differently by members of the stable and unstable cultures. Natives of the stable context tended to hold a view of the research mission that extended far beyond the adjoining city, while the members of the unstable context preferred to preserve the traditional localized community orientation that had characterized their strongly held commitment to urban service. Differences in presidential articulation of collective norms was also apparent—*excellence* was stressed in the stable culture, while *quality* received the official corporate nod in the unstable context. Differing levels of collective acceptance regarding each theme distinguished the two university contexts as well. Once researchers have isolated salient cultural dimensions, the extent of penetration in the values, negotiated rules, and tangible artifacts of an organizational context then needs to be determined in order for patterns of unity and differentiation to emerge.

Although initially developed in a university context, the *Organizational Dimensions Survey* (ODS) may provide a starting point from which to trace penetration of cultural dimensions in organizational contexts outside of academe. The dimensions forming the theoretical conceptualization of the scale reflect tendencies of societal groups to form collective orientations regarding the variability of human nature, amount of control over the environment, perceptions of time and activity, and power distribution in relationships. The eighteen items of the ODS representing dimensions of vision, mission, tradition, destiny, and productivity describe several universal organizational concerns and are relevant to corporate or nonprofit contexts.

In order to advance development of an organizational culture construct beyond its initial descriptive stages to a more refined level of evaluation and augmentation, researchers need to compare empirical studies that have isolated core cultural dimensions across a variety of diverse contexts. Since this investigation was exploratory in nature, the ODS needs to be tested in other contexts by performing confirmatory factor analysis to validate cultural dimensions and to determine if the reliability will remain consistent. Comparisons between the dimensions in this study and those isolated by other researchers help to build a compendium of core unitary value orientations that cross contextual boundaries and that serve to advance our definition of organizational culture.

Instruments like the ODS developed in this investigation also may potentially serve as useful diagnostic tools for administrative officers in contemporary organizations, facilitating the discovery of shared employee perceptions and illuminating areas of diversity. Such knowledge can assist administrators in goal setting and strategic planning efforts, as well as in the creation of print and oral persuasive messages targeted to specific subcultural groups (e.g., in-house employee publications). By taking the time to accurately assess patterns of cultural unity and differentiation across an organizational context, leaders in succession stage growth cultures may be able to achieve a greater degree of success in launching their ambitious programs of cultural transformation.

Another area of challenge in future studies is the charting of the historical penetration of organizational culture through content analysis of artifacts. Future content analyses of university publications might use the dimensions isolated in this investigation as the basis for coding categories. An option that may strengthen the analysis of historical penetration of cultural constructs would be the use of print records other than major university publications. For instance, Kreps (1980) used recordings and transcripts of faculty senate meetings to test Weick's (1979) concept of equivocality in group decision making. Local press coverage of university news over a specified time period could provide a more unbiased perspective of salient cultural dimensions. Interviews with university employees at the administrative and staff levels, in which they would recall critical incidents in the history of the organization, could potentially lend a unique perspective to analyzing historical cultural penetration.

As we have illustrated in the study, the researcher needs to consider how the penetration of core dimensions serves to either unify or differentiate members of a particular culture. An analysis of the functional outcomes of culture could prove useful in gauging the benefits or liabilities inherent in organizations exhibiting strong unitary cultures or in more loosely coupled systems that may thrive on diverse subcultural orientations. Functional outcomes traditionally associated with unitary cultures, such as commitment, productivity, efficiency, or effectiveness, may actually be a paradoxical blend of cultural dimensions that support both integration and differentiation within that context. In addition, the exploration of contexts that are strengthened by value differentiation will assume greater prominence as employers seek to increase multicultural diversity in their workforces.

Rather than focusing on the benefits of cultural differentiation, organizational research tends to be dominated by "strong" culture models that oversimplify the relationship of cohesive cultures to key outcome variables, such as performance. Saffold (1988) noted several erroneous assumptions inherent in many studies guided by "strong culture hypotheses." Most investigations that link organizational culture with performance assume a unitary culture that is largely dependent on existing "excellent" composite culture profiles. Cultural strength is often imprecisely defined, resulting in the use of inadequate methodologies to assess the breadth of shared conceptualizations.

Corrective measures include more precision in assessing penetration of cultural constructs and symbolic potency across levels of the organization. An adequate "cultural-performance" framework should also examine how shared conceptualizations contribute to several critical processes related to performance. These factors include: climate formation, behavioral control, strategy formulation, social efficiency, organizational learning, integration/differentiation, and leadership. Saffold's (1988) prescription for more precise cultural measurement is consistent with the holistic approach presented in this volume, because it represents a cross-paradigmatic perspective. Unitary culture approaches with their emphasis on cohesion across organizational ranks could be enriched greatly by an exploration of how diverse subcultures may actually strengthen certain contexts.

Finally, future studies need to explore more fully the interrelationships among organizational culture, commitment, and identification. Because this investigation used a version of the *Organizational Identification Questionnaire* (Cheney 1983a) that did not tap maintaining membership, future investigations might profitably use the full twenty-five-item version. Also, dimensions of identification and commitment (pride, similarity, emotional attachment, membership) need to be studied in relation to dimensions of organizational culture isolated in this investigation. A comparative study analyzing results from the *Organizational Dimensions Survey*, the *Organizational Identification Questionnaire*, and the *Organizational Commitment Questionnaire* (Mowday, Steers & Porter 1979) could assist researchers in determining relationships among organizational culture, identification, and commitment.

Since levels of organizational identification within stable and unstable cultures were almost identical in this investigation, the measurement of "cultural identification," could prove to be a more fruitful avenue of exploration. Perhaps stable cultures are characterized not only by widespread collective agreement regarding core cultural constructs, but also by high levels of identification with these salient cultural dimensions. The development of a measure to determine employee identification with unitary cultural dimensions, such as those isolated in this investigation (vision, mission, tradition, destiny, and productivity) may prove to be a way of assessing organizational culture identification.

THE PATH TO FUTURE RESEARCH AGENDAS

Although researchers in search of organizational culture "diverge" along distinct functional and interpretive "paths" in their journey through dense corporate "woods," the explorers do concur on one common compass point—the complexity of analyzing cultural contexts. For example, Pettigrew (1990) summarized several analytical issues that make organizational cultures difficult to study or to change. The fact that culture is a multilevel construct that may be approached at a highly abstract, metaphoric layer or at a more tangible artifactual level increases analytic difficulty. Also, organizational levels may complicate an analysis of an entire organization in terms of shared conceptualizations. Most investigations are capable of only microanalyses that capture cultural snapshots of a distinct workplace group. The interdependency of interfacing cognitive conceptual systems increases the difficulty of obtaining a clear-cut map of an organization's multiple cultures. Additionally, political issues and ethical implications, affecting both the perpetuation of corporate culture and the maintenance of distinct work unit cultures, also contribute to analytic complexity.

In order to cope with complexity dilemmas, several researchers have generated agendas containing pertinent issues that need to be addressed if organizational culture is to continue its development as a construct. Our discussion centers around three challenging areas that will serve to enhance the present state of organizational culture research: primacy of the communication process, potential in strategic failures, and emergence of ethical concerns. The first dominant theme that could enrich organizational culture research agendas is the importance of the communication process as the prime means of creating, maintaining, or repairing organizational cultures. Although much attention is devoted to what culture is, or the factors that compose certain types of cultures, the dynamic interaction process underlying cultural generation in organizations is largely overlooked.

Secondly, much research focuses on models of organizational excellence or quality, while cultural shortcomings, as evidenced in strategic failures, are rarely analyzed in depth. In the midst of organizational failures or crises, the effects of distinct cultural orientations may be illuminated with greater clarity. Thirdly, the ethical responsibilities of culture creators is an area that will be receiving more attention in the future. As critical researchers bring to light potential destructive implications of imposed corporate cultures, there will be an increased demand for an explication of cultural models that foster employee voice and promote individual empowerment through collectively negotiated ideologies.

Primacy of Communication in Culture Creation

Researchers can approach the process of communication from either a mechanistic standpoint by focusing on the channels transmitting cultural information or by observing natives engaged in symbolic interaction to collectively negotiate cultural norms and rituals. For instance, in their communication agenda for organizational culture research, Sypher, Applegate, and Sypher (1985) suggest that workplace investigators determine how communication abilities impact on employee accomodation to cultural demands. Another pertinent topic involves how different interaction patterns affect the development and nature of organizational cultures. Finally, the analysis of interpersonal and group relations is another area that may be enriched by a clearer understanding of the role of communication in creating, maintaining, or repairing an organization's culture. For instance, intergroup conflict or communication breakdowns in superior-subordinate interaction may have roots in value clashes (Schein 1985; Rokeach 1973). The role of communication in development of multiple workplace cultures, and in the resolution of conflict arising from a clash of disparate subcultural values and norms remain key issues for further research.

Analytic Potential in Strategic Failures

In his rationale for why culture should be better understood, Schein (1985) suggested that the effects of an organization's culture on strategy is an important area of consideration in the planning process. Analyzing historical case studies of organizations may shed light on how certain cultural dimensions spawn strategic failures. For example, the failure of mergers, acquisitions, and diversifications may stem from an ignorance of existing shared asssumptions operant in a particular context. Collective resistance to change that constrains planned innovations, as was evident in the unstable university culture, may emanate directly from the values of an organization's dominant culture or countercultural groups. Also, the failure to integrate new technologies may be a direct result of strongly held norms and values that inhibit acceptance. More careful "level" assessment of an organization's culture also assists in pinpointing where socialization problems tend to occur. If an individual or group complies with certain norms, but ultimately rejects more deeply rooted ideological concepts guiding the organization's mission, then the identification process will remain unfinished. Goal setting across organizational divisions, from personnel functions to management operations, can be enhanced by more sophisticated analyses of strategic shortcomings over time.

An organization that recently experienced a crisis that called into serious question existing contextual assumptions, norms, and operational strategies, is the highly publicized Rochester Institute of Technology affair with the Central Intelligence Agency. In the words of one local reporter, the plot centers around the question, "Can a university be true to its responsibilities as an academic institution while maintaining strong ties to a covert, investigative arm of the federal government?" Media coverage referred to the case as a saga of a university's "courtship and marriage with a controversial government agency" that spins a tale of intrigue, revealing "how a university is governed, who defines policy, who determines curriculum, and where loyalties are." The university's involvement with the CIA became a public concern, because the University's president had facilitated the establishment and growth of a private research corporation that was not subject to academic oversight. The crisis heated up when it was revealed that RIT's president had "delayed being specific" about taking a sabbatical leave to work for the CIA. (See News Coverage Citations: Astor, 1991, Towler, 1991).

A wide array of seemingly covert administrative strategic goals were revealed to the public as an independent investigation of university policy was conducted by a panel of RIT faculty members, trustees, students, and alumni. The senior fact finder of the investigative panel, a legal studies professor from another academic institution, criticized the fact that a relationship between the CIA and the university had been allowed to flourish without adequate knowledge of the whole academic community. During his term, the president actively increased the amount and scope of classified government research conducted on campus and did this without full knowledge and approval of the university's faculty, deans, and board of trustees. One member of the fact-finding committee painted a shocking picture of the university administration as "characterized by episodes of autocratic management, secrecy, lack of candor, intimidation, and slander on the part of some; and of fearfulness, irresponsibility, and indifference on the part of others."

Further, the investigative work of the committee appeared to be hindered by administrative document shredding. The investigative panel recommended several strategic alterations, including suspending or terminating some CIA operations at the university and instituting new policies and procedures to ensure proper academic oversight of classified research. With an administration's policy failures illuminated in the heat of a crisis, as was the case with the RIT-CIA situation, organizational analysts can more easily trace cultural roots of strategic management problems. The case also provides a classic example of ethical considerations involving leadership and maintenance of cultural contexts, which will be discussed in the next section.

Emergence of Ethical Concerns

As the RIT-CIA case example illustrates, examining the moral and political significance of organizational life should assume a prominent position in any future research agenda. An area of concern for researchers and consultants alike is the ethical dimension of encouraging managers to more actively engage in "framing" contexts and in shaping interpretive schemes (Smircich 1983b). The consequences of leaders' capacity to induce "cognitive redefinition" by "articulating and selling new visions and concepts" (Schein 1985) needs to be examined within an ethical frame. Consistent with critical theory, Smircich encouraged organizational consultants to use more "self reflective" models that reveal the social construction of power relationships.

In the RIT-CIA case, the ethical question is: can the university maintain its relationship to the covert agency and meet its academic responsibilities to students and faculty members? In responding to this question, the investigative panel concluded that a university's essential mission to promote open inquiry and free expression of ideas and information stands in stark opposition to the CIA's function of secrecy. With the former president's resignation, the new appointee will be immersed in a culture experiencing an unstable succession stage. As we have noted in the university study reported in the previous two chapters, the new leader has the option of either imposing a transactional management stance by attempting to establish control over artifactual and normative cultural elements or electing a transformational leadership approach to collectively articulate a new university vision. The new president could read the crisis as merely a case of adverse publicity that requires strategic control measures to reinstate cultural stability. However, more ethical cultural approaches would rely on transformational leadership techniques that would allow the RIT community to become collectively involved in charting a new course for the university.

Social forecasters have predicted a "triumph of the individual" (Naisbitt & Aburdene 1990) as an important trend that will shape organizations of the future. Similarly, trends in organizational administration portend a gradual but consistent shift away from a management paradigm grounded in control, toward a more ethical new leadership paradigm characterized by cooperation and facilitation. Organizational culture research will reflect this increased ethical vigilance by generating more investigations that focus on how leaders empower individuals in the collective creation of contextual value orientations. With a prevailing management paradigm that focuses on order and control, organizational structures or ideologies may systematically hinder members' involvement in open discourse (Forester 1983). However, implementation of a "culture for coaching" (Evered & Selman 1989) is one way to empower workers by increasing free expression and encouraging innovation. This human relations-oriented "coaching style" decreases worker alienation by allowing listening to assume a more prominent position in the culture of the organization. Rather than promoting control as a primary cultural dimension in an organizational context, the "coaching" approach encourages management-employee partnerships. In light of these trends, it seems safe to predict that fewer studies will focus on "gaining control" of corporate generated cultures; rather, more investigations will trace leadership patterns of collective empowerment that serve to generate shared organizational ideologies.

A theme that helps to synthesize the future directions presented in this chapter is that the primary function of a culture construct is in merging organizational reality with collective vision. Leaders in contemporary organizations need to take a close look at the essential dimensions that form distinct patterns of assumptions, norms, and values across their contexts. Studying an organization's cultural map that graphically displays unification and diversity, can provide leaders with a consistent reality check, so essential before embarking on a course of strategic innovation. The future challenge for organizations lies in the creation of ethical managerial partnerships that view their primary mission as one of facilitating cultural transformation that is constantly reaching toward a collective vision.

PART III

PART III

APPENDIX A

RESEARCH HYPOTHESES, PHASES, AND VARIABLES

Phase Two: Survey	*Independent Variables*	*Dependent Variables*
Psychological Penetration		
Employees in stable and unstable cultures will differ in their perception of culture.	Culture stability	Cultural dimensions
Employees in stable cultures will have higher levels of organizational identification than employees in unstable cultures.	Culture stability	Identification
Sociological Penetration		
Administration, faculty, and staff level employees will differ in their perception of culture.	Organization level	Cultural dimensions
Administration, faculty, and staff level employees in a stable culture will differ in their perception of culture from employees in an unstable culture.	Organization level Culture stability	Cultural dimensions

Administration, faculty, and staff level employees will differ in organizational identification.	Organization level	Identification
Employees at the career stages of socialization, performance, and outcome will differ in their perception of culture and identification.	Career stages	Cultural dimensions Identification

Phase Three: Content Analysis

Historical Penetration

In stable cultures, the projection of culture, as depicted in print communications, will remain consistent over time.	Time periods	Cultural dimensions
In unstable cultures, the projection of culture, as depicted in print communications, will change over time.	Time periods	Cultural dimensions

APPENDIX B

INTERVIEW SCHEDULE

C 1. If you were asked to describe the university (in general) to someone from outside this area, what would you say?

C 2. In your estimation, what is the most important part of the University's mission?

A 3. How anxious is the university community to carry out the mission?

R 4. For you personally and/or professionally, what is the greatest advantage gained by working here? Greatest disadvantage?

C 5. How would you describe the "culture" of this place?

T 6. Who could best tell the university's "story?"

R 7. In general, what does a person need to know to function successfully on the administrative staff?

R 8. What type of individual would not "fit-in" well at this university?

A 9. Would you describe the "tempo" of the university as "hyper-active" or "laid-back?" Other?

T 10. To what extent is the university tradition-minded?

T 11. What changes have you noticed since you've been a part of the university?

T 12. Would you call this university innovative? In what ways? If not, why?

A 13. To what extent is the university satisfied with where it is now?

A 14. What kind of decisions take a long time to make? Why? What kinds of decisions are made more quickly?

T 15. How important is precedent in decision making?

H 16. Does the university reward individual initiative?

R 17. How would administrators feel if a faculty/staff member would bypass his/her immediate superior to complain about a problem?

R 18. If a faculty/staff member had a suggestion for making the university better, what channels would he/she use? Could someone walk right into the president's office?

E 19. What constituencies outside the university influence decisions?

E 20. To what extent is the university able to shape its own future?

E 21. Consider the relationship of the university with its important external constituencies. Who is the "mover and shaker?" Who is the "puppet?"

E 22. What kind of influence does the university have in this community?

H 23. Do you think most of the employees here put in a good day's work? Why? Why not?

H 24. Has the university become too lenient with tenure?

H 25. Are most people at this university sufficiently committed to the organization?

H 26. Do you have any kind of formal future planning for employees? If so, what type, and at what levels? (ie. retirement, pension)

H 27. Besides specific requirements in a job description, what qualities do you look for in recruitment of future employees?

H 28. Do you have, in printed form, any type of employee guidelines concerning rights and/or ethics?

H 29. What is the nature of your grievance policy?

C 30. If you had to give a speech to a group of alumni, what information about the university would you consider essential to share with them about the current state of the university?

C 31. What other university most clearly resembles yours? Why?

C 32. Are there any well-known anecdotes concerning university life in general which are often shared among employees?

Notes: Letter Code in parentheses indicates cultural dimension tapped by the question.

H = Human Nature
E = Environment
T = Time
A = Activity
R = Relational
C = Culture (university)

APPENDIX C

CODING CATEGORIES FOR INTERVIEW AND CONTENT ANALYSIS
DATA WITH CODING INSTRUCTIONS

(based on five dimensions of cultural value orientations)

Category 1. Orientation Toward Human Nature: Good—Variable—Evil

HNG
: Human Nature Good
  - statements having to do with praising the achievements of individuals or groups, encouraging individual initiative

HNV
: Human Nature Variable
  - statements acknowledging levels of variability in regard to human nature

HNE
: Human Nature Evil
  - statements that stress the need to restrain or limit the power or responsibility of individuals due to their own innate ignorance, laziness, or lack of skill

NA
: Not Applicable

Category 2. Orientation to the Environment: Subjugaiion—Harmony—Control

ENSUB
: Environmental Subjugation
  - statements describing how external constituencies prevent the organization from achieving its potential
  - outside forces are constraining or controlling the functioning of the organization

ENHAR
: Environmental Harmony

- statements describing how the organization achieves mutually satisfying decisions with outside constituencies
- all parties involved work together, no one group wields a significant amount of power

ENCON   Environmental Control
- statements that describe the organization in a leadership role in dealing with outside constituencies
- the organization possesses more power in negotiations than the outside constituencies

NA   Not Applicable

Category 3. Orientation Toward Time: Past—Present—Future

TPA   Time Past
- statements stressing the value of tradition in regard to the organization encouraging a return to symbols or rituals utilized in the organization's history

TPR   Time Present
- statements stressing the need for the organization to deal with the challenges of daily living rather than going back to old methods or looking toward an uncertain future

TF   Time Future
- statements dealing with future plans/visions for the organization
- the mobilization of resources for future endeavors

NA   Not Applicable

Category 4. Orientation Toward Activity: Passive—Moderate—Active

PAS   Passive
- statements exhibiting a very cautious approach to innovation
- a high level of uncertainty avoidance in organizational decisions
- low risk-taking

MOD   Moderate
- statements showing some risk-taking weighted against an assessment of possible losses

ACT   Active
- statements revealing high risk-taking
- low level of uncertainty avoidance
- movement toward innovation

NA   Not Applicable

Category 5. *Orientation Toward Relationships (Power Distribution):
Lineality—Consultative—Collaterality*

RLIN   Relational Lineality
              • statements expressing the value of using proper channels
                when communicating with others in the organization
              • an emphasis on autocratic leadership styles
              • relationships determined mainly by roles/placement on
                organizational chart
              • high power distance
              • decisions best made by individuals high in chain of
                command

RCON   Relational Consultative
              • statements based on assumption that all levels in the orga-
                nization have relevant information to contribute, but
                power remains in hands of leaders
              • moderate power distance

RCOL   Relational Collaterality
              • statements expressing the value of team work
              • group/participative decision making
              • low levels of power distance
              • democratic management styles
              • collegiality shared power base
              • administration and employees share responsibility for
                organizational decisions

NA   Not Applicable

CODING PROCEDURES

Coding Instructions for Interview Data

The following guidelines are used after transcribing interview statements on
cards. Read the statements individually and analyze each statement using
guidelines #1 through #6.

1.   Does the statement describe an *orientation toward human nature?*

      Using the coding categories in this appendix, determine whether the
      statement fits into the *human nature good* (HNG), human nature variable
      (HNV) or *human nature evil* (HNE) category. Place the card in the
      appropriate pile.

If the statement cannot be placed into a coding option in category 1, then proceed to #2.

2.   Does the statement describe an *orientation to the environment?*

Using coding categories in this appendix, determine whether the statement fits into the *environmental subjugation* (ENSUB), environmental harmony (ENHAR) or *environmental control* (ENCON) category. Place the card in the appropriate pile.

If the statement cannot be placed into a coding option in category 2, then proceed to #3.

3.   Does the statement describe an *orientation toward time?*

Using the coding categories in this appendix, determine whether the statement fits into the *time past* (TPA), time present (TPR) or *time future* (TF) category. Place the card in the appropriate pile.

If the statement cannot be placed into a coding option in category 3, then proceed to #4.

4.   Does the statement describe an *orientation toward activity?*

Using the coding categories in this appendix, determine whether the statement fits into *activity passive* (PAS), activity moderate (MOD) or *activity active* (ACT) category. Place the card in the appropriate pile.

If the statement cannot be placed into a coding option in Category 4, then proceed to #5.

5.   Does the statement describe an *orientation toward relationships?*

Using the coding categories in this appendix, determine whether the statement fits into the *relational lineality* (RLIN), relational consultative (RCON) or *relational collaterality* (RCOL) category. Place the card in the appropriate pile.

If the statement cannot be placed into a coding option in category 5, then proceed to #6.

6.   If the statement refers to a specific aspect of the university, place it in a sixth category (university).

Sort the university statements into four categories :

   a. Statements describing university *teaching, research* or *service* as a *local mission.*
   b. Statements describing university *teaching, research,* or *service* as a *national mission.*

    c. Statements describing a *shared culture.*
    d. Statements describing a *lack of shared culture*—statements emphasizing *diversity* of the university.

After the sorting procedure has been completed, eliminate statements that did not fit into the 6 categories, or statements that lacked clarity, then proceed to #7.

7. Analyze the statements in each coding category for similarities and group similar statements together.

8. Count the number of similar statements in each coding category, and select the 3 most frequently mentioned themes in each coding option.

Coding Instructions for Content Analysis Data

General Guidelines

1. Read each article 6 times—once for general meaning and once for each of the five coding categories:
    a. Orientation toward human nature
    b. Orientation to the environment
    c. Orientation toward time
    d. Orientation toward activity
    e. Orientation toward relationships

(see descriptions of coding options for each category in this appendix).

2. Give each article 5 codes—one for each of the cultural value orientations (listed above).

3. If the content of the article could be coded in more than one category, select the category that best fits the overall theme of the article.

Procedures

1. Begin coding by reading the entire article for general meaning. Look carefully at the headline to grasp the dominant thematic content of the article.

2. Then, beginning with category 1, read the entire article to determine if it contains material describing a *good, variable,* or *evil orientation toward human nature* (see coding category descriptions).
If there are no statements in the article pertaining to a good, variable, or evil human nature orientation, then assign a code of NA (not applicable) for this category.

3. Proceeding to category 2, read the article to locate material pertaining to a *subjugation, harmony,* or *control orientation to the environment.* If

there are no statements in the article pertaining to the environment orientation, assign a code of NA (not applicable) for this category.

4.   Follow the same procedure as described above for category 3, *orientation toward time*. Read the article for statements pertaining to a *past, present,* or *future* orientation toward time. Select the category that best fits the overall theme of the article. If no material in the article describes a past, present, or future orientation toward time, then assign the article a code of NA (not applicable) for this category.

5.   As you have for the three previous categories, read the entire article for statements pertaining to *orientation toward activity*. Assign a code of either *passive, moderate,* or *active* orientation toward activity. Select the category that best fits with the overall theme of the article. If no material in the article pertains to this orientation, assign a code of NA (not applicable).

6.   Continue the coding procedure by reading the article for material describing category 5, an *orientation toward relationships*. Assign a code of either *lineality, consultative,* or *collaterality*, selecting the one category that best describes the overall thematic content of the article. If none of the categories are appropriate, assign a code of NA (not applicable) for this category.

ODS Items in Cultural Dimension Categories

Human Nature Orientation 1 (evil) ————(good) 5	M	SD
1. **There is a problem here with apathetic employees.**	3.03	1.12
* 2. **Our staff is industrious; the work ethic is very much alive here.**	3.51	1.03
* 3. Faculty members do their utmost to carry out the university's mission.	3.31	0.83
4. Administators fail to appreciate the efforts of faculty and staff.	2.91	1.14
5. **Certain faculty members are unproductive.**	2.15	0.86
* 6. **We have many capable people in administrative posts.**	3.55	1.07

Environmental Orientation 1 (subjugation) ————(control) 5		
* 1. **The university plays a major role in the well-being of the community.**	4.36	0.81
2. **Groups outside the university have too much to say about how the institution is run.**	3.36	0.90
3. Problems with state funding pose a threat to our well being.	3.13	1.14
* 4. Politically, we have a lot of clout in the legislative process.	2.96	0.93

* 5. **The university is able to shape its own future without undue constraints from outside forces.**   2.73   1.01

6. **It seems as if the university is at the mercy of the state when making decisions.**   2.65   0.99

Time Orientation   1 (past)————(future) 5

1. A lot of people would like to see things done the way they used to be.   2.98   0.98

* 2. **The whole university is moving in a positive direction.**   3.93   0.97

* 3. **We are emerging as a future-oriented university.**   3.93   0.89

* 4. **Future planning is very important at this university.**   4.13   0.81

* 5. **There is a shared perception of vibrant growth and change.**   3.42   1.03

6. **Traditions are important to this university.**   3.09   0.94

Activity Orientation   1 (passive)————(active) 5

* 1. **Our university is probably more innovative than most.**   3.38   1.08

* 2. **The university is significantly more active than in the past; we're definitely "on the move."**   4.10   0.91

3. We have a fairly "laid back" tempo in most departments.   3.21   0.96

4. This administration is overly cautious.   3.69   0.81

5. The university is slow and careful in its planning.   2.93   0.92

* 6. Our style at the university is action oriented; we're willing to take risks.   3.30   0.91

Relational Orientation   1 (lineality)————(collaterality) 5

1. At this university, it is important to address people by their proper titles   3.06   1.05

2. People aren't consulted before decisions are made.   2.77   1.09

3. Lines of authority are clear here.   2.50   0.99

4. Going over the head of one's superior rarely happens here.   2.80   0.92

5. People who like to "give orders" fit in well here.	3.20	0.99
* 6. This environment emphasizes teamwork rather than individual "stars."	2.99	1.05

University Dimension   1 (service)————(research) 5
(Mission)   local_____national

* 1. We need to hire more "big names" to foster a national reputation.	2.92	1.21
2. **Educating our undergraduates from surrounding areas is our primary reason for being in operation.**	2.98	1.21
3. Teaching and community service are enough for granting of tenure here.	3.97	0.97
4. As a public university, we have the obligation to develop the economic base of the local community.	2.23	0.93
* 5. **One of our primary activities is securing external funding for faculty research.**	3.76	1.01
* 6. Efforts to build a national reputation for this university have been centered primarily on nonacademic activities.	3.12	1.33

Shared Culture   1 (diversity) ———— (collectivity) 5

1. **The university is still groping for a tradition.**	3.03	1.05
* 2. **Most people here would agree that we're respected by other institutions.**	3.58	0.93
* 3. Even though this is a large institution, we manage to keep a family spirit.	2.72	1.07
4. **The university lacks tradition.**	3.21	1.15

Note: Means and standard deviations represent entire sample with missing cases deleted (N = 411).
*indicates items coded on the scale (orientations of good, control, future, active,collaterality, research, national, collectivity)

- Bolded statements indicate 20-item ODS

OIQ ITEMS IN COMPONENTS OF IDENTIFICATION CATEGORIES

Similarity	M	SD
1. In general, people employed by the university are working toward the same goals.	3.26	1.00
2. In general, I view the university's problems as my problems.	3.02	1.08
3. I have a lot in common with others employed by the university.	3.51	0.92
4. I find that my values and the university's values are similar.	3.12	1.00
5. I find it easy to identify myself with the university.	3.71	1.01
Pride		
1. I am proud to be an employee of the university.	4.11	0.90
2. The university's image in the community represents me well.	3.57	1.00
3. I often describe myself to others by saying, "I work for the university."	3.93	0.99
4. I talk up the university to my friends as a great place to work.	3.63	1.15
5. I become irritated when I hear others outside the university criticize the institution.	3.34	1.14

Emotional Attachment

1. I feel that the university cares about me.   2.95   1.14

2. I have warm feelings toward the university as a
    place to work.   3.64   1.08

3. My association with the university is only a small
    part of who I am. *   2.72   1.15

4. I feel very little loyalty to the university.*   3.87   1.09

5. I really care about the fate of the university.   4.27   0.82

Notes: Means and standard deviations represent the entire sample with
    missing cases deleted ($N = 438$).
* Recoded items

SUMMARY OF STEPWISE MULTIPLE DISCRIMINANT ANALYSIS

Summary Statistics

Canonical Correlation:	.61	Chi-square: 192.52	
Eigenvalue:	.60	$df = 5$	
Wilk's Lambda:	.63	$sig = p < .001$	

Step	Dependent Variables	Wilk's Lambda	Coefficients Function	Structure
1	Mission	.68	.86	.88*
2	Tradition	.67	-.27	-.16
3	Vision	.65	.64	.27*
4	Identification	.63	-.40	.02
5	Destiny	.63	-.18	-.18
	Productivity	X		-.09

Group Centroids:

Group 1 (unstable)	-.80
Group 2 (stable)	.74

Percentage of Cases Correctly Classified

Group 1 ($N = 204$)	78.4%
Group 2 ($N = 217$)	77.0%
Total Cases ($N = 421$)	77.7%

Note 1: $p < .001$.
Note 2: X = Variables not meeting Wilk's Lambda criteria for stepwise selection.

REFERENCES

Adams, G. B., & Ingersoll, V. H. (1985). The difficulty of framing a perspective on organizational culture. In P. J. Frost, L. F. Moore, M. R. Louis, C. C. Lundberg, & J. Martin (Eds.), *Organizational culture* (pp. 223–234). Beverly Hills: Sage.

Adizes, I. (1988). *Corporate lifecycles.* Englewood Cliffs, NJ: Prentice-Hall.

Akin, G., & Hopelain, D. (1988). Finding the culture of productivity. In *Organizational Dynamics Special Reports: Corporate Culture* (pp. 127–140). New York: American Management Association.

Adler, N. J., & Jelinek, M. (1986). Is "Organization Culture" culture bound? *Human Resource Management, 25,* 73–90.

Argyris, C., & Schon, D. (1978). *Organizational learning: A theory of action perspective.* Reading, MA: Addison-Wesley.

Atkinson, P. E. (1990). *Creating culture change: The key to successful total quality management.* Bedford, UK: IFS Publications.

Babbie, E. R. (1973). *Survey research methods.* Belmont, CA: Wadsworth.

Bacharach, S. B. (1989). Organizational theories: Some criteria for evaluation. *Academy of Management Review, 14,* 496–515.

Barley, S.R. (1983). Semiotics and the study of occupational and organizational cultures. *Administrative Science Quarterly, 28,* 393–413.

Barnett, G. A. (1988). Communication and organizational culture. In G. M. Goldhaber & G. A. Barnett (Eds.), *Handbook of organizational communication* (pp. 101–130). Norwood, NJ: Ablex.

Bartunek, J. M. (1988). The dynamics of personal and organizational reframing. In R.E. Quinn & K. S. Cameron (Eds.), *Paradox and transformation:*

Toward a theory of change in organization and management (pp. 137–62). Cambridge, MA: Ballinger.

Beck, B. E. F., & Moore, L. F. (1985). Linking the host culture to organizational variables. In P. J. Frost, L. F. Moore, M. R. Louis, C. C. Lundberg, & J. Martin (Eds.), *Organizational culture* (pp. 335–54). Beverly Hills,: Sage.

Berg, P. (1985). Organization change as a symbolic transformation process. In P. J. Frost, L. F. Moore, M. R. Louis, C. C. Lundberg, & J. Martin (Eds.), *Organizational culture* (pp. 281–300) Beverly Hills.: Sage.

Berger, P. L., & Luckmann, T. (1966). *The social construction of reality.* Garden City, NY: Doubleday.

Bettinger, C. (1989). Use corporate culture to trigger high performance. *Journal of Business Strategy, 10,* 38–42.

Bock, P. K. (1988). *Rethinking psychological anthropology.* New York: Freeman.

Boje, D.M., Fedor, B., & Rowland, M. (1982). Mythmaking: A qualitative step in OD interventions. *Journal of Applied Behavioral Science, 18,* 17–28.

Bolman, L. G., & Deal, T. E. (1991). *Reframing organizations: Artistry, choice, and leadership.* San Francisco: Jossey-Bass.

Bormann, E. G. (1983) Symbolic convergence: Organizational communication and culture. In L. L. Putnam & M. E. Pacanowsky (Eds.), *Communication and organizations: An interpretive approach* (pp. 99–122). Beverly Hills: Sage.

Bormann, E. G., Howell, W., Nichols, R., & Shapiro, G. (1982). *Interpersonal communication in the modern organization* (2nd ed.). Englewood Cliffs, NJ: Prentice-Hall.

Bougon, M. G., Weick, K. E., & Binkhorst, D. (1977). Cognition in organizations: An analysis of the Utrecht Jazz Orchestra. *Administrative Science Quarterly, 22,* 606–39.

Broms, H., & Gahmberg, H. (1983). Communication to self in organizations and cultures. *Administrative Science Quarterly, 28,* 482–95.

Brown, M. (1983, November). *That reminds me of a story: Speech action in organizational socialization.* Paper presented at the annual meeting of the Speech Communication Association, Washington, DC.

Brown, M. E. (1969). Identification and some conditions of organizational involvement. *Administrative Science Quarterly, 14,* 346–55.

Brown, M. H., & McMillan, J. J. (1991). Culture as text: The development of an organizational narrative. *The Southern Communication Journal, 57,* 49–60.

Brucker, E. (1985). Managing the university for excellence. In J. Blits (Ed.), *The American university* (pp. 121–35). Buffalo, NY: Prometheus.

Buchanan, B. (1974). Building organizational commitment: The socialization of managers in work organizations. *Administrative Science Quarterly, 19,* 533–46.

Bullis, C. (1990, June). *Organizational transformation through values: A comparison of unitary and pluralist perspectives.* Paper presented at the annual meeting of the International Communication Association, Dublin, Ireland.

Bullis, C., & Bach, B. (1986, November). *Attributions associated with specific turning points in the development of the individual-organization relationship.* Paper presented at the annual meeting of the Speech Communication Association, Chicago.

Burke, K. (1950). *A rhetoric of motives.* Berkeley: University of California Press.

Burns, J. M. (1978). *Leadership.* New York: Harper & Row.

Burrell, G., & Morgan, G. (1979). *Sociological paradigms and organizational analysis: Elements of the sociology of corporate life.* London: Heinemann.

Cameron, K., & Whetten, D. A. (1981). Perceptions of organization effectiveness across organization life cycles. *Administrative Science Quarterly, 26,* 525–44.

Cameron, K. S. (1986a.) A study of organizational effectiveness and its predictors. *Management Science, 32,* 87–112.

———. (1986b.) Effectiveness as paradox. *Management Science, 32,* 539–53.

Cameron, K. S., & Quinn, R. E. (1988). Organizational paradox and transformation. In R. E. Quinn & K. S. Cameron (Eds.). *Paradox and transformation: Toward a theory of change in organization and management* (pp.1–18) Cambridge, MA: Ballinger.

Caplow, T. (1983). *Principles of organization.* New York: Harcourt Brace.

Carnegie Commission on Higher Education. (1972). *The campus and the city: Maximizing assets and reducing liabilities.* New York: McGraw-Hill.

———. (1973). *The purposes and the performance of higher education in the United States: Approaching the year 2000.* New York: McGraw–Hill.

Carroll, D. (1983). A disappointing search for excellence. *Harvard Business Review,* 78–88.

Cheney, G. (1983a). On the various and changing means of organizational membership: A field study of organizational identification. *Communication Monographs, 50,* 242–62.

———. (1983b). The rhetoric of identification and the study of organizational communication. *Quarterly Journal of Speech, 69,* 143–58.

———. (1986, November). *Prelude to the study of identity networks.* Paper presented at the annual meeting of the Speech Communication Association, Chicago.

Cheney, G., & Tompkins, P. K. (1987). Coming to terms with organizational identification and commitment. *Central States Speech Journal, 38,* 1–15.

Child, J. (1981). Culture, contingency and capitalism in the cross-national study of organizations. In L. L. Cummings & B. M. Staw (Eds.), *Research in organizational behavior* (pp. 303–56). Greenwich, CT: JAI Press.

Clark, B. R. (1972). The organizational saga in higher education. *Administrative Science Quarterly, 17,* 178–84.

Cohen, J. (1977). *Statistical power analysis for the behavioral sciences.* New York: Academic Press.

Conway, J. A. (1985). A perspective on organizational cultures and organizational belief structure. *Educational Administration Quarterly, 21,* 7–25.

Cooke, R. A., & Lafferty, J. C. (1986). *Level V: Organizational culture inventory-Form III.* Plymouth, MI: Human Synergistics.

Cooke, R. A., & Rousseau, D. M. (1988). Behavioral norms and expectations: A quantitative approach to the assessment of organizational culture. *Group and Organization Studies, 13,* 245–73.

Cronbach, L. J. (1951). Coefficient alpha and the internal structure of tests. *Psychometrika, 16,* 407–24.

Cummings, L. L. (1983). The logics of management. *Academy of Management Review, 8,* 539–46.

Cushman, D. P., King, S. S., & Smith, T. (1988). The rules perspective on organizational communication research. In G. M. Goldhaber & G. A. Barnett (Eds.), *Handbook of organizational communication* (pp. 55–94). Norwood, NJ: Ablex.

Czarniawska-Joerges, B. (1992). *Exploring complex organizations: A cultural perspective.* Newbury Park, CA: Sage.

Daft, R. (1983). Symbols in organizations: A dual-content framework for analysis. In L. R. Pondy, P. J. Frost, G. Morgan, & T. C. Dandridge

(Eds.), *Organizational symbolism* (pp. 199–206). Greenwich, CT: JAI Press.

Dandridge, T. C. (1983). Symbols' function and use. In L. R. Pondy, P. J. Frost, G. Morgan, & T. C. Dandridge (Eds.), *Organizational symbolism* (pp. 69–80). Greenwich, CT: JAI Press.

Dandridge, T. C., Mitroff, I. I., & Joyce, W. (1980). Organizational symbolism: A topic to expand organizational analysis. *Academy of Management Review, 5,* 248–56.

Dansereau, F., & Alutto, J. A. (1990). Level-of-analysis issues in climate and culture research. In B. Schneider (Ed.), *Organizational climate and culture* (pp. 193–236) San Francisco: Jossey-Bass.

Deal, T. E., & Kennedy, A. A. (1982). *Corporate cultures: The rites and rituals of corporate life.* Reading, MA: Addison-Wesley.

Deetz, S. (1982). Critical interpretive research in organizational communication. *Western Journal of Speech Communication, 46,* 131–49.

Deetz, S., & Huspek, M. (1990, June). *Evaluating and reforming corporate culture: Critical communication theory as a moral foundation for investigating micro power practices.* Paper presented at the annual meeting of the International Communication Association, Dublin, Ireland.

Deetz, S. A. (1985). Ethical considerations in cultural research in organizations. In P. J. Frost, L. F. Moore, M. R. Louis, C. C. Lundberg, & J. Martin (Eds.), *Organizational culture* (pp. 253–70) Beverly Hills: Sage.

Deetz, S. A. & Kersten, A. (1983). Critical models of interpretative research. In L. L. Putnam & M. E. Pacanowsky (Eds.), *Communication and organizations: An interpretative approach* (pp. 147–71). Beverly Hills: Sage.

Denison, D. R. (1990). *Corporate culture and organizational effectiveness.* New York: Wiley.

Denzin, N. K. (1978). *The research act.* New York: McGraw-Hill.

Duncan, R., & Weiss, A. (1979). Organizational learning: Implications for organizational design. In B. M. Staw (Ed.), *Research in organizational behavior* (pp. 75–124). Greenwich, CT: JAI Press.

Dyer, W. G. (1985). The cycle of cultural evolution in organizations. In R. H. Kilmann, M. J. Saxton, & R. Serpa (Eds.), *Gaining control of the corporate culture* (pp. 200–29). San Francisco: Jossey-Bass.

Emery, F. E., & Trist, E. L. (1972). *Towards a social ecology: Contextual appreciation of the future in the present.* London: Plenum.

Enz, C. (1988) The role of value congruity in intraorganizational power. *Administrative Science Quarterly, 33*, 284–304.

Evan, W. M. (1975). Measuring the impact of culture on organizations. *International Studies on Management and Organization, 50*, 91–113.

Evered, R. (1983). The language of organizations: The case of the Navy. In L. R. Pondy, P. J. Frost, G. Morgan, & T. C. Dandridge (Eds.), *Organizational symbolism* (pp. 125–43). Greenwich, CT: JAI Press.

Evered, R., & Louis, M. R. (1981). Alternative perspectives in the organizational sciences: Inquiry from the inside and inquiry from the outside. *Academy of Management Review, 6*, 385–96.

Evered, R. D., & Selman, J. C. (1989). Coaching and the art of management. *Organizational Dynamics, 18*, 16–32.

Feldman, D. C. (1981). The multiple socialization of organization members. *Academy of Management Review, 6*, 309–18.

Fisher, W. R. (1984). Narration as a human communication paradigm: The case of public moral argument. *Communication Monographs, 51*, 1–22.

―――. (1985). The narrative paradigm: An elaboration. *Communication Monographs, 52*, 347–64.

Fitzgerald, T. H. (1988). Can change in organizational culture really be managed? *Organizational Dynamics, 17*, 5–15.

Forester, J. (1983). Critical theory and organizational analysis. In G. Morgan (Ed.), *Beyond method: Strategies for social research* (pp. 234–46), Newbury Park, CA: Sage.

Frake, C. O. (1972). The ethnographic study of cognitive systems. In J. P. Spradley (Ed.), *Culture and cognition: Rules, maps, and plans* (pp. 191–205). San Francisco: Chandler.

Francis, D., & Woodcock, M. (1990). *Unblocking organizational values*. Glenview, IL: Scott, Foresman.

Frost, P. J., Moore, L. F., Louis, M. R., Lundberg, C. C., & Martin, J. (Eds.) (1991). *Reframing organizational culture*. Newbury Park, CA: Sage.

Fry, S. L. (1992). Getting the private sector to give. *Public Relations Journal, 48*, 5.

Garsombke, D. J. (1988). Organizational culture dons the mantle of militarism. *Organizational Dynamics, 17*, 46–56.

Geertz, C. (1973). *The interpretation of cultures*. New York: Basic Books.

Gioia, D. A., & Pitre, E. (1990). Multiparadigm perspectives on theory building. *Academy of Management Review, 15*, 584–602.

Glaser, S. R., Zamanou, S., & Hacker, K. (1987, May). *Measuring and interpreting organizational culture.* Paper presented at the annual meeting of the International Communication Association, Montreal.

Goetz, J. P., & LeCompte, M. D. (1984). *Ethnography and qualitative design in educational research.* Orlando, FL: Academic Press.

Goffman, E. (1956). *The presentation of self in everyday life.* New York: Doubleday.

Goodall, A. L., Wilson, G. L., & Waagen, C. (1986). The performance appraisal interview: An interpretive reassessment. *Quarterly Journal of Speech, 72,* 74–87.

Gorden, W. I. (1984, May–June). Organizational imperatives and cultural modifiers. *Business Horizons,* pp. 76–83.

Gorden, W. I., & Infante, D. A. (1991). Test of a communication model of organizational commitment. *Communication Quarterly, 39,* 144–55.

Gregory, K. L. (1983) Native view paradigms: Multiple cultures and culture conflicts. *Administrative Science Quarterly, 28,* 359–76.

Hall, D. T., Schneider, B., & Nygren, H. T. (1970). Personal factors in organizational identification. *Administrative Science Quarterly, 15,* 176–89.

Harris, L., & Cronen, V. E. (1979). A rules-based model for the analysis and evaluation of organizational communication. *Communication Quarterly, 27,* 12–28.

Harris, M. (1981). *Cultural materialism.* New York: Crowell.

Harris, R., & DuMond, S. (1990). *The excellence audit: A tactical guide to support your management revolution.* Palo Alto, CA: Publishing Power.

Herskowitz, M. J. (1948). *Man and his works.* New York: Knopf.

Hitt, M. A., & Ireland, R. D. (1987). Peters and Waterman revisited: The unended quest for excellence. *Academy of Management Executive, 2,* 91–98.

Hofstede, G. (1980). *Culture's consequences.* Beverly Hills: Sage.

Hofstede, G., Neuijen, B., Ohayv, D. D., & Sanders, G. (1990). Measuring organizational cultures: A qualtiative and quantitative study across twenty cases. *Administrative Science Quarterly, 35,* 286–316.

Holsti, O. R. (1969). *Content analysis for the social sciences and humanities.* Reading, MA: Addison-Wesley.

Jablin, F. M. (1982). Organizational communication: An assimilation approach. In M. Roloff & C. Berger (Eds.), *Social cognition and communication* (pp. 255–86). Beverly Hills: Sage.

Jick, T. D. (1979). Mixing qualitative and quantitative methods: Triangulation in action. *Administrative Science Quarterly, 24,* 602–11.

Johnson, B., Natarajan, A., & Rappaport, A. (1985). Shareholder returns and corporate excellence. *Journal of Business Strategy, 6,* 52–62.

Jones, G. R. (1986). Socialization tactics, self-efficacy, and newcomers' adjustments to organizations. *Academy of Management Journal, 29,* 262–79.

Jung, C. G. (1964). *Man and his symbols.* New York: Dell.

Kelly, G. A. (1955). *The psychology of personal constructs.* New York: Norton.

Kelman, H. C. (1958). Compliance, identification and internalization: Three processes of attitude change. *Journal of Conflict Resolution, 2,* 51–60.

Kerr, J., & Slocum, J. W., Jr. (1987). Managing corporate culture through reward systems. *Academy of Management Executive, 1,* 99–108.

Kilmann, R. H. (1985). Five steps for closing culture gaps. In R. H. Kilmann, M. J. Saxton, & R., Serpa (Eds.), *Gaining control of the corporate culture* (pp. 351–69). San Francisco: Jossey-Bass.

Kilmann, R. H., & Saxton, M. J. (1983). *The Kilmann-Saxton culture-gap survey.* Pittsburgh: Organizational Design Consultants.

Kinkead, R. W., & Winokur, D. (1991). Navigating the seas of cultural change. *Public Relations Journal, 47,* 14–21.

Kissler, G. D. (1991). The change riders: Managing the power of change. Reading, MA: Addison-Wesley.

Kluckhohn, C. (1951). Values and value orientations in the theory of action. In T. Parsons & E. Shils (Eds.), *Toward a general theory of action* (pp. 409–11) Cambridge, MA: Harvard University Press.

Kluckhohn, F. R., & Stodtbeck, F. L. (1961). *Variations in value orientations.* New York: Row, Peterson.

Kopelman, R. E., Brief, A. P., & Guzzo, R. A. (1990). The role of climate and culture in productivity. In B. Schneider (Ed.), *Organizational climate and culture* (pp. 282–318). San Francisco: Jossey-Bass.

Krefting, L. A., & Frost, P. J. (1985). Untangling webs, surfing waves, and wildcatting: A multiple-metaphor perspective on managing organizational culture. In P. J. Frost, L. F. Moore, M. R. Louis, C. C. Lundberg, & J. Martin (Eds.), *Organizational culture* (pp. 155–68). Beverly Hills: Sage.

Kreps, G. L. (1980). A field experimental test and reevaluation of Weick's model of organizing. In D. Nimmo (Ed.), *Communication yearbook 4* (pp. 389–400). New Brunswick, NJ: Transaction Books.

————. (1983) The use of interpretive research to develop a socialization program at RCA. In L. L. Putnam & M. E. Pacanowsky (Eds.), *Communication and organizations: An interpretive approach* (pp. 243–56), Beverly Hills: Sage.

————. (1986). *Organizational communication theory and practice.* New York: Longman.

Kroeber, A. L., & Parsons, T. (1958). The concept of culture and of social system. *American Sociological Review, 23,* 582–83.

Kuhn, T. S. (1970). *The structure of scientific revolutions.* Chicago: University of Chicago Press.

Lafferty, J. C. (1973). *Level I: Life styles inventory self-description.* Plymouth, MI: Human Synergistics.

Lawrence, P. R., & Lorsch, J. W. (1967). Differentiation & integration in complex organizations. *Administrative Science Quarterly, 12,* 1–47.

Lee, S. M. (1971). An empirical analysis of organizational identification. *The Academy of Management Journal, 14,* 213–226.

Liedtka, J. M. (1989). Value congruence: The interplay of individuals and organizational value systems. *Journal of Business Ethics, 8,* 805–15.

Limerick, D. C. (1990). Managers of meaning: From Bob Geldof's Band Aid to Australian CEO's. *Organizational Dynamics, 18,* 22–33.

Lincoln, Y. S. (Ed.), (1985). *Organizational theory and inquiry: The paradigm revolution.* Beverly Hills: Sage.

Lord, R. G., & Kernan, M. C. (1987). Scripts as determinants of purposeful behavior in organizations. *Academy of Management Review, 12,* 265–77.

Louis, M. R. (1980). Surprise and sense-making: What newcomers experience in entering unfamiliar organizational settings. *Administrative Science Quarterly, 25,* 226–51.

————. (1983). Organizations as culture-bearing milieux. In L. R. Pondy, P. J. Frost, G. Morgan, & T. C. Dandridge (Eds.), *Organizational symbolism* (pp. 39-54). Greenwich, CT: JAI Press.

————. (1985a). An investigator's guide to workplace culture. In P. J. Frost, L. F. Moore, M. R. Louis, C. C. Lundberg, & J. Martin (Eds.), *Organizational culture* (pp. 73–94). Beverly Hills: Sage.

————. (1985b). Sourcing workplace cultures: Why, when, and how. In R. H. Kilmann, M. J. Saxton, & R. Serpa (Eds.), *Gaining control of the corporate culture* (pp. 126–36). San Francisco: Jossey-Bass.

————. (1990) Acculturation in the workplace: Newcomers as lay ethnographers. In B. Schneider (Ed.), *Organizational climate and culture* (pp. 85–129). San Francisco: Jossey-Bass.

Lundberg, C. (1985). On the feasibility of cultural intervention in organizations. In P. J. Frost, L. F. Moore, M. R. Louis, C. C. Lundberg, & J. Martin (Eds.), *Organizational culture* (pp. 169–86). Beverly Hills: Sage.

McGregor, D. (1960). *The human side of enterprise.* New York: McGraw-Hill

Martin, J., Feldman, M. S., Hatch, M. J., & Sitkin, S. B. (1983). The uniqueness paradox in organization stories. *Administrative Science Quarterly, 28,* 438–53.

Martin, J., & Powers, M. (1983). Truth or corporate propaganda: The value of a good war story. In L. R. Pondy, P. J. Frost, G. Morgan, & T. C. Dandridge (Eds.), *Organizational symbolism* (pp. 93–108). Greenwich, CT: JAI Press.

Martin, J. & Siehl, C. (1988). Organizational culture and counterculture: An uneasy symbiosis. *Organizational Dynamics Special Reports: Corporate Culture* (pp. 77–89). New York: American Management Association.

Martin, J., Sitkin, S. B., & Boehm, M. (1985). Founders and the elusiveness of a cultural legacy. In P. J. Frost, L. F. Moore, M. R. Louis, C. C. Lundberg, & J. Martin (Eds.), *Organizational culture* (pp. 99–124). Beverly Hills: Sage.

Meyerson, D. E. (1991). Acknowledging and uncovering ambiguities in cultures. In P. J. Frost, L. F. Moore, M. R. Louis, C. C. Lundberg, & J. Martin (Eds.), *Reframing organizational culture* (pp. 254–70). Newbury Park: Sage.

Meyerson, D. E., & Martin, J. (1987). Cultural change: An integration of three different views. *Journal of Management Studies, 24,* 623–47.

Miller, V., Allen, M., Casey, M., & Johnson, J. R. (1990, June). *A factor analytic investigation of the organizational identification questionnaire instrument.* Paper presented at the annual meeting of the International Communication Association, Dublin, Ireland.

Mintzberg, H. (1983). *Power in and around organizations.* Englewood Cliffs, NJ: Prentice-Hall.

Mirvis, P. H. (1985). Managing research while researching managers. In P. J. Frost, L. F. Moore, M. R. Louis, C. C. Lundberg, & J. Martin (Eds.), *Organizational culture* (pp. 201–21). Beverly Hills: Sage.

Mitroff, I. I. (1983). *Stakeholders of the organizational mind.* San Francisco: Jossey-Bass.

Morgan, G. (1980). Paradigms, metaphors, and puzzle solving in organization theory. *Administrative Science Quarterly, 25,* 605–22.

———. (1983). Research strategies. In G. Morgan (Ed.). *Beyond method: Strategies for social research* (pp. 19–42). Newbury Park, CA: Sage.

———. (1986). *Images of organization.* Beverly Hills: Sage.

Morgan, G., Frost, P. J., & Pondy, L. R. (1983). Organizational symbolism: An overview. In L. R. Pondy, P. J. Frost, G. Morgan, & T. C. Dandridge (Eds.), *Organizational symbolism* (pp. 3–38). Greenwich, CT: JAI Press.

Mowday, R. T., Steers, R. M., & Porter, L. W. (1979). The measurement of organizational commitment. *Journal of Vocational Behavior, 14,* 224–47.

Mumby, D. (1987). The political function of narratives in organizations. *Communication Monographs, 54,* 113–27.

Nair, K. (1988). *Beyond winning: The handbook for the leadership revolution.* Phoenix, AZ: Paradox.

Naisbitt, J. (1982). *Megatrends: Ten new directions transforming our lives.* New York: Warner.

Naisbitt, J., & Aburdene, P. (1990). *Megatrends 2000: Ten new directions for the 1990's.* New York: Avon.

Neisser, V. (1976). *Cognition and reality: Principles and implications of cognitive psychology.* San Francisco: Freeman.

Nord, W. R. (1985). Can organizational culture be managed? A synthesis. In P. J. Frost, L. F. Moore, M. R. Louis, C. C. Lundberg, & J. Martin (Eds.) *Organizational culture* (pp. 187–96). Beverly Hills: Sage.

Olins, W. (1989). *Corporate identity: Making business strategy visible through design.* Boston: Harvard Business School Press.

O'Reilly, C. A., Chatman, J., & Caldwell, D. F. (1991). People and organizational culture: A profile comparison approach in assessing person-organization fit. *The Academy of Management Journal, 34,* 487–516.

O'Toole, J. J. (1979). Corporate and managerial cultures. In C. Cooper (Ed.), *Behavioral problems in organizations* (pp. 7–28) Englewood Cliffs, NJ: Prentice-Hall.

Ouchi, W .G. (1980). Markets, bureaucracies, and clans. *Administrative Science Quarterly, 25,* 129–41.

Ouchi, W. G. (1981). *Theory Z.* Reading, MA: Addison-Wesley.

Owens, R. G., & Steinhoff, C. R. (1989). Towards a theory of organizational culture. *Journal of Educational Administration, 27,* 6–16.

Pacanowsky, M. E., & O'Donnell-Trujillo, N. (1983). Organizational communication as cultural performance. *Communication Monographs, 50,* 126–47.

Patchen, M. (1970). *Participation, achievement, and involvement on the job.* Englewood Cliffs, NJ: Prentice-Hall.

Peters, T. J. (1988). *Thriving on chaos: Handbook for a management revolution.* New York: Harper & Row.

Peters, T. J., & Waterman, R. (1982). *In search of excellence.* New York: Harper & Row.

Pettigrew, A. (1979). On studying organizational cultures. *Administrative Science Quarterly, 24,* 570–81.

Pettigrew, A. M. (1990). Organizational climate and culture: Two constructs in search of a role. In B. Schneider (Ed.), *Organizational climate and culture* (pp. 413–34), San Francisco: Jossey-Bass.

Pfeffer, J. (1981). Management as symbolic action: The creation and maintenance of organizational paradigms. In L. L. Cummings & B. M. Staw (Eds.), *Research in organizational behavior* (Vol. 3, pp. 1–52). Greenwich, CT: JAI Press.

Phair, J. T. (1992). Education report card. *Public Relations Journal, 48(2)* 22–24.

Pondy, L. R. (1983). The role of metaphors and myths in organization and in the facilitation of change. In L. R. Pondy, P. J. Frost, G. Morgan, & T. C. Dandridge (Eds.), *Organizational symbolism* (pp. 157–66). Greenwich, CT: JAI Press.

Pondy, L. R., Frost, P. J., Morgan, G., & Dandridge, T. C. (Eds.) (1983). *Organizational symbolism.* Greenwich, CT: JAI Press.

Porter, L. W., Crampton, W. J., & Smith, F. J. (1976). Organizational commitment and managerial turnover: A longitudinal study. *Organizational Behavior and Human Performance, 15,* 87–98.

Porter, L. W., Steers, R. M., Mowday, R. T., & Boulian, P. V. (1974). Organizational commitment, job satisfaction, and turnover among psychiatric technicians. *Journal of Applied Psychology, 59,* 603–9.

Putnam, L. L. (1982). Paradigms for organizational research: An overview and synthesis. *Western Journal of Speech Communication, 46,* 192–206.

———. (1983). The interpretative perspective: An alternative to functionalism. In L. L. Putnam & M. E. Pacanowsky (Eds.), *Communication and organizations: An interpretive approach* (pp. 13–30). Beverly Hills: Sage.

Quinn, R. E., & Cameron, K. S. (1988). Paradox and transformation: A framework for viewing organization and management. In R. E. Quinn & K. S. Cameron (Eds.), *Paradox and transformation: Toward a theory of change in organization and management* (pp. 289–308). Cambridge, MA: Ballinger.

Quinn, R. E., & McGrath, M. R. (1985). The transformation of organizational cultures: A competing values perspective. In P. J. Frost, L. F. Moore, M. R. Louis, C. C. Lundberg, & J. Martin (Eds.), *Organizational culture* (pp. 315-334). Beverly Hills: Sage.

Radcliffe-Brown, A. (1952). *Structure and function in primitive society.* London: Cohen & West.

Reichers, A. E. (1985). A review and reconceptualization of organizational commitment. *Academy of Management Review, 10,* 465–76.

Reichers, A. E., & Schneider, B. (1990). Climate and culture: An evolution of constructs. In B. Schneider (Ed.), *Organizational climate and culture* (pp. 5–39). San Francisco: Jossey-Bass.

Reynolds, P. (1987, March). Imposing a corporate culture. *Psychology Today,* pp. 33–38.

Riley, P. (1983). A structurationist account of political cultures. *Administrative Science Quarterly, 28,* 414–37.

Rokeach, M. (1973). *The nature of human values.* New York: Free Press.

Rosengren, K. E. (1986). Media linkages between culture and other societal systems. In M. L. McLaughlin (Ed.), *Communication yearbook 9* (pp. 19–56). Beverly Hills: Sage.

Rousseau, D. M. (1990). Assessing organizational culture: The case for multiple methods. In B. Schneider (Ed.), *Organizational climate and culture* (pp. 153–92). San Francisco: Jossey-Bass.

Sackmann, S. A. (1991). *Cultural knowledge in organizations: Exploring the collective mind.* Newbury Park, CA: Sage.

Saffold, G. S. (1988). Culture traits, strength and organizational performance: Moving beyond strong culture. *Academy of Management Review, 13,* 546–57.

Sathe, V. (1985). How to decipher and change corporate culture. In R. H. Kilmann, M. J. Saxton, & R. Serpa (Eds.), *Gaining control of the corporate culture.* (pp. 230–61). San Francisco: Jossey-Bass.

Schall, M. S. (1983). A communication rules approach to organizational culture. *Administrative Science Quarterly, 28,* 557–81.

Schein, E. H. (1985). *Organizational culture and leadership.* San Francisco: Jossey-Bass.

———. (1990). Organizational culture. *American Psychologist, 45,* 109–19.

———. (1991). What is culture? In P. J. Frost, L. F. Moore, M. R. Louis, C. C. Lundberg, & J. A. Martin (Eds.), *Reframing organizational culture* (pp. 243–53). Newbury Park, CA: Sage.

Schwartz, H., & Davis, S. M. (1988). Matching corporate culture and business strategy. *Organizational Dynamics Special Reports: Corporate Culture* (pp. 1–20). New York: American Management Association.

Scott, W. (1955). Reliability of content analysis: The case of nominal scale coding. *Public Opinion Quarterly, 19,* 321–25.

Sethia, N. K., & Von Glinow, M. A. (1985). Arriving at four cultures by managing the reward system. In R. H. Kilmann, M. J. Saxton, & R. Serpa (Eds.), *Gaining control of the corporate culture* (pp. 400–20). San Francisco: Jossey-Bass.

Siehl, C. (1985). After the founder: An opportunity to manage culture. In P. J. Frost, L. F. Moore, M. R. Louis, C. C. Lundberg, & J. Martin (Eds.), *Organizational culture* (pp. 125–40). Beverly Hills: Sage.

Siehl, C. & Martin, J. (1988). Measuring organizational culture: Mixing qualitative and quantitative methods. In M. O. Jones, M. D. Moore, & R. C. Snyder (Eds.), *Inside organizations: Understanding the human dimension* (pp. 79–104). Newbury Park, CA: Sage.

Siehl, C., & Martin, J. (1990). Organizational culture: A key to financial performance? In B. Schneider (Ed.), *Organizational climate and culture* (pp. 241–81), San Francisco: Jossey-Bass.

Smircich, L. (1983a). Concepts of culture and organizational analysis. *Administrative Science Quarterly, 28,* 339–58.

———. (1983b). Implications for management theory. In L. L. Putnam & M. E. Pacanowsky (Eds.), *Communication and organizations: An interpretive approach* (pp. 221–41). Beverly Hills: Sage.

———. (1983c). Organizations as shared meanings. In L. R. Pondy, P. J. Frost, G. Morgan, & T. C. Dandridge (Eds.), *Organizational symbolism* (pp. 55–65). Greenwich, CT: JAI Press.

———. (1983d). Studying organizations as cultures: Organization as a network of meaning. In G. Morgan (Ed.), *Beyond method: Strategies for social research* (pp. 160–72). Newbury Park: Sage.

———. (1985). Is the concept of culture a paradigm for understanding organizations and ourselves? In P. J. Frost, L. F. Moore, M. R. Louis, C. C. Lundberg, & J. Martin (Eds.), *Organizational culture* (pp. 55–72). Beverly Hills: Sage.

Smircich, L., & Calás, M. B. (1987). Organizational culture: A critical assessment. In F. M. Jablin, L. L. Putnam, K. H. Roberts, & L. W. Porter (Eds.), *Handbook of organizational communication* (pp. 228–63). Newbury Park, CA: Sage.

Spradley, J. P. (Ed.) (1972). *Culture and cognition: Rules, maps, and plans.* San Francisco: Chandler.

Steers, R. M. (1977). Antecedents and outcomes of organizational commitment. *Administrative Science Quarterly, 22,* 46–56.

Steinhoff, C. R., & Owens, R. G. (1989). The organizational culture assessment inventory: A metaphorical analysis in educational settings. *Journal of Educational Administration, 27,* 17–23.

Stohl, C. (1986). The role of memorable messages in the process of organizational socialization. *Communication Quarterly, 34,* 231–49.

Sypher, B. D., Applegate, J. L., & Sypher, H. E. (1985). Culture and communication in organizational contexts. In W. B. Gudykunst, L. P. Stewart, & S. Ting-Toomey (Eds.), *Communication, culture, and organizational processes* (pp. 13–29). Beverly Hills: Sage.

Thompson, K. R., & Luthans, F. (1990). Organizational culture: A behavioral perspective. In B. Schneider (Ed.), *Organizational climate and culture* (pp. 319–44). San Francisco: Jossey-Bass.

Tichy, N. M. (1980). Problem cycles in organizations and the management of change. In J. R. Kimberly and R. H. Miles (Eds.), *The organization-*

al life cycle (pp.164–83). San Francisco: Jossey-Bass.

Tierney, W. G. (1988). Organizational culture in higher education: Defining the essentials. *Journal of Higher Education, 59,* 2–21.

Tompkins, P. K., Fisher, J. Y., Infante, D. A., & Tompkins, E. L. (1975). Kenneth Burke and the inherent characteristics of formal organizations: A field study. *Speech Monographs, 42,* 135–42.

Treadwell, D. F. (1987, May). *Organizational communication and image of the organization.* Paper presented at the annual meeting of the International Communication Association, Montreal.

Trice, H. M., & Beyer, J. M. (1984). Studying organizational cultures through rites and ceremonials. *Academy of Management Review, 9,* 653–69.

Turner, S. (1977). Complex organizations as savage tribes. *Journal for the Theory of Social Behavior, 7,* 99–125.

Van Ess Coeling, H., & Wilcox, J. R. (1988). Understanding organizational culture: A key to management decision making. *Journal of Nursing Administration, 18,* 16–23.

Van Maanen, J. (1975). Breaking in: Socialization to work. In R. Dubin (Ed.), *Handbook of work, organization and society* (pp. 67–120). Chicago: Rand McNally.

Van Maanen, J., & Barley, S. R. (1985). Cultural organization: Fragments of a theory. In P. J. Frost, L. F. Moore, M. R. Louis, C. C. Lundberg, & J. Martin (Eds.), *Organizational culture* (pp. 31–53). Beverly Hills: Sage.

Van Maanen, J., & Schein, E. (1979). Toward a theory of organizational socialization. In B. M. Staw (Ed.), *Research in organizational behavior* (Vol. 1, pp. 209-264). Greenwich, CT: JAI Press.

Wacker, G. J. (1981). Toward a cognitive methodology of organizational assessment. *Journal of Applied Behavioral Science, 17,* 114–29.

Weick, K. E. (1976). Educational organizations as loosely coupled systems. *Administrative Science Quarterly, 21,* 1–19.

———. (1979). *The social psychology of organizing.* Reading, MA: Addison-Wesley.

Whyte, W. H. (1955). *Street Corner Society.* Chicago: University of Chicago Press.

Wilkins, A. L. (1983a). The culture audit: A tool for understanding organizations. *Organizational Dynamics, 4,* 24–38.

———. (1983b). Organizational stories as symbols which control the organization. In L. R. Pondy, P. J. Frost, G. Morgan, & T. C. Dandridge (Eds.), *Organizational symbolism* (pp. 81–92). Greenwich, CT: JAI Press.

Wilkins, A. L., & Patterson, K. J. (1985). You can't get there from here: What will make culture-change projects fail. In R. H. Kilmann, M. J. Saxton, & R. Serpa (Eds), *Gaining control of the corporate culture* (pp. 262–91). San Francisco: Jossey-Bass.

Wilkins, A. L., & Ouchi, W. G. (1983). Efficient cultures: Exploring the relationship between culture and organizational performance. *Administrative Science Quarterly, 28,* 468–81.

NEWS COVERAGE CITATIONS

Astor, W, (1991, November 27). To shred is human: to forgive is too. *City Newspaper,* Rochester, NY., pp. 3–5.

Deutsch, C. H. (1991, December 15). Call it CEO disease, then listen. *New York Times,* p. 23.

Sabath, D. (1992, March 5). A focus on listening—Manager Linda Miller shares quality time with Ford Plant Staff. *The Cleveland Plain Dealer,* p. 1, Section F.

Staff. (1992, March 24). Frank Perdue's son building new company image. *The Cleveland Plain Dealer,* p. 9.

Towler, M.A. (1991, November 27). Spy story: The CIA and RIT. *City Newspaper,* Rochester, NY., pp. 3–5.

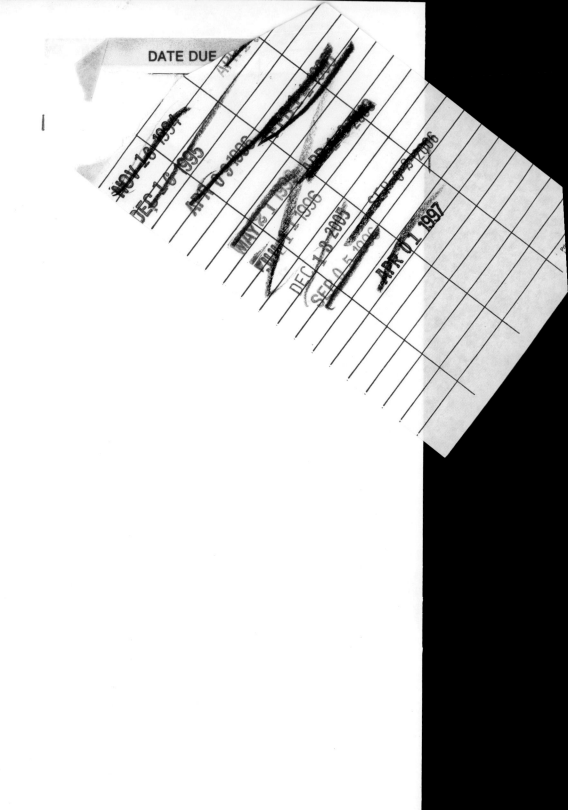

DATE DUE

NOV 18 1994

DEC 18 1995

APR 09 1996

MAY 3 1 1996

DEC 18 2005

SEP 0 5 1996

APR 01 1997